LEARNING ORGANIZATIONAL BEHAVIORS HOW BRING

ECONOMIC BENEFITS

JOHN LOK

Copyright

Contents

Contents

Preface

Behavioral economy is one useful and fun social subject. Behavioral economists ususally research how and why human behaviors may influence economy growth or recession, or how and why economy environment changing factor may influence human behavior changes.

This book concerns how to apply how behavioral economic and psychological methods to attempt to explain whether your organization can be influenced to raise your employee individual productive efficiency as well as improve service performance to achieve to let your clients feel more satisfaction by effective human resource training or/and facility management methods. My research questions include:Can effective human resource training or/and facility management influences your organization's employee individual productive efficiency raising and/or service performance improving?Can effective workplace working environment facility management influence your organization's employee individual emotion and working attitude to be changed more positive to raise productive efficiency and/or service performance? Can effective human resource training program improve your organization's employee individual skill level in order to raise productive efficiency and/or service performance? Has it relationship between effective human resource training and facility management to influence organization's employee individual productive efficient level and service performance in long term?

I shall apply psychological method to attempt to recommend whether it is the right time to your organization ought need to find methods to raise your organization's human resource trai8ning course(s) quality and/or improve your organization's facility management in-house service quality to let your employees feel more comfortable to work in your organization's any working environment in order to achieve the raising productive efficiency and/or improving service performance consequence in possible.

This book divides three parts. The first part indicates how organizations can attempt to apply different psychological methods to research how and why employee individual selects to do the behavioral performance in organizations in order to let any organization leaders can judge whether it is right time that whose organization ought need to attempt to change human resource training courses quality in order to let employees' skills can be improved more effectively and/or applying facility management to be implemented more comfortable to let employees to feel in order to achieve the productive efficient raising and/or the service performance improving possible consequence in long term.

The second part indicates to explain whether effective human resource training courses can help to raise employee productive efficiency and/or improve service performance. I shall indicate the whole HRM successful elements to explain whether it can still help the organization to raise employee efficiency and/or improve service performance, if the organization neglects to implement an effective human resource training course program to let whose employees to attempt to learn any work-related skills.

The final part indicates whether organization's facility management in-house department or outsourced department can achieve to improve its office or warehouse working environment to be more comfortable to let employees to feel in order to influence their productive efficiencies to be raised or improving their service performance to bring customers' more satisfactory feeling.

I write this book aims to hope any organization leaders can attempt to apply psychological methods to predict whether their in-house facility management service is enough or/and human resource management strategy and training course program strategies which both have relationship to influence their employees' productive efficiency and service performance in order to achieve aim to raise more satisfactory feeling to their customers. I believe that effective facility management can improve better workplace environment to influence employee individual productive efficiency raising as well as effective human resource training course program can improve employee individual service performance in order to achieve customers to feel more satisfactory service performance in consequence for the organization's service.

Whether do any organizations need facility management department? What function of benefits will bring when the organization sets up one facility management department? If the organization lacked one facility management department, what the disadvantage it will bring to influence the organization's operation? Does it has relationship between raising efficiency or improving performance and facility management department?

I shall indicate some evidences and causations to explain what will be occured when the organizatin owns one facility management department or it lacks one facility management department in its organization. Any readers can make judgement whether in what suitations , the organization needs to set up one facility management department in order to bring advantages or waste essential human resource or raise service cost from the facility management department.

Prologue

Table of contents

CHAPTER I

How to apply psychological methods to predict employee individual productive efficiency and service performance

It has one interesting question concerns whether organization's in-house training management and/or human resource training course program has close relationship to influence the reducing or raising employee individual productive efficiency and better or worse service performance consequence. I shall recommend that any organizations can apply psychological methods to judge whether they need to implement their facility management department to change their working environment to be better in order to let their employees feel comfortable to work to raise productive efficiency or implement training course program to let employees to learn in order to raise productive efficiency.

How to apply psychological methods to evaluate whether the organization has need to implement in-house facility management service and/or any employee train courses program? I shall explain as below:

Some essential concepts in psychological research concerns employees' raising productive efficiency and improving service performance may include as below:

Cause means something which results in an effect, e.g. The organization's employees overall service performance is worse (effect) and/or overall productive efficiencies are worse (effect), it is due to the poor working environment factor and/or lacking effective training courses program provision (cause).

Action or condition means that the organization's employees often perform worse (action), it is due to they feel worse working environment (condition) to influence their emotions are negative.

Data means that the information from which are drawn and conclusions reached. For example, the organization gather much data concerns workplace environment variable facilities factors, e.g. enough air conditioners, clean canteen facilities, large warehouse space allocation available etc. variable data as well as training course contents data. Then it will analyze all these both kinds of data to make the accurate conclusion reached to make the more accurate conclusion reached to judge whether its employees overall worse productive efficiencies and/or worse service performance effect is due to either worse workplace working environment and/or lacking enough training work-related course programs provision to let them to learn.

In any large organization's improving employee performance and/or raising productive efficient research. A lot of data are collected in numerical form , e.g. how many employees feel their workplace environment is satisfactory or comfortable? The workplace environment comfortable and satisfactory feeling rank:

1 means the most comfortable,
2 means more comfortable,
3 means worse comfortable,
4 means the worst comfortable,

But it is equally viable to use data in the form of text for an analysis and randomized experiment means a type of research in which participants in research are allocated at random by chance to an experimental or control condition. For example, when one organization needs 20 employees to do one performance improving experiment in one day 9 working hours. The 10 employees are arranged to manufacture watch product in one large warehouse space available and more cool temperature feeling working environment factory. The other 10 employees are arranged to manufacture the same kind of watch product in one small warehouse space available and less cool temperature feeling working environment factory. Hence, their watch manufacturing skills must be same proficient level, due to they manufacture the same kind of watch and the two factories' equipment supplies are same number and their qualities are the new purchase, and these two factories' worker number is same , the two variable factors are different , it is only that one factory's space is large size and the another factory's space is small size as well as one factory's temperature is much cooler, but the another factory's temperature is less cooler. This organization's one day working hours experiment aims to research whether these two factories' warehouses' space size variable factor and temperature variable factor whether they can influence these two groups of 20 workers overall productive efficiencies to bring the much difference of watch manufacturing number of the day. For example, if the large space available and much cooler warehouse's 10 employees can manufacture more than 500 watch number in the day. Otherwise, the small space available and less cooler warehouse's 10 employees can only manufacture less than 300 watch number in the day. Then, the organization can judge the conclusion concerns whether the better or worse workplace environment will influence its employee individual emotion to manufacture its watch number.

All above these elements are each employee performance psychological research needs. Any employee psychological researches are needed to evaluate the evidence. Employee individual performance psychology is not simply about learning what conclusions have been reached on a particular topic. It is perhaps more important to find out and carefully evaluate the evidence which has led to these conclusion. For example, in the newspapers and on television, one comes findings from advertising influence consumers (audiences) media research. IS it simply to accept what the newspaper or television report claims or world it be better media choice to be advertised to check the original research in order to evaluate what the best advertisement media choice to attract customers (audiences') attention actually meant?

The evaluation of employee performance improving evidence involves examining the general findings that the employee psychological research is making about an issue and the information or data that are relevant to this finding, e.g. The organization has not implement any training courses to let employee to learn, (it is the issue), the organization discovers many employee individual productive efficiency is worse, it is the information, this organization will gather different variable data, e.g. the equipment number whether is enough to supply to them to apply to work, the equipment quality whether is good or bad, new or old, the worker individual proficient skill level is high or low or their working related skillful experience is long or short years. Then, it can make more accurate analysis to find whether the lacking enough training courses program to be supplied to let them to learn any work-related skills, whether this variable factor is the major variable factor to influence their performance to be worse. For example, if this organization had enough equipment number supply and all are new and these workers' overall proficient skillful level is high and they own many years working experience about this kind of tasks. Then, it can judge the lacking training course program implementation is not the major factor to influence their performance to be worse, due to their performance ought not need to be improved. SO, it ought have other variable factors to influence their performance to be worse suddenly.

Then, the organization needs to check whether the evidence or data support the finding or whether the finding goes beyond what could be confidently concluded. However, in any employee performance psychological research, there is nothing wrong with speculation as such since hypotheses.

What is causal explanation in employee performance psychological research view point? Dennis , H & Duncan, C. (2005, pp.9-10), they stated one prisoner suicide risk case example of causal explanation, a psychologist who wishes to predict suicide risk in prisoners does not have to know why the causes of suicide among prisoners. So, if research shows that being in prison for the first time is the strongest predictor of suicide, then this is a possible predictor. It is irrelevant whether the predictor is in itself the direct cause of suicide. Hence, the two authors assume that in general, the prisoners choose to suicide in prisons. Usually, they are the first time to enter the prison. Because the two authors assume the psychologist does not know what the reasons cause prisoners choose to do suicide behavior in prison, because it is possible that these first time prisoners who feel difficult to adapt to live in prisons' strange environment, they afraid to be fright or hurt by another/other prisoners' hurt in prison, they also feel alone , when they can not live with their families together forever. SO, the reasons of not adaptable living in prison, which is possible to cause the first time prisoners to choose to suicide in prisons. Hence, the first time prisoners suicide in prisons, it is one assumption , when the psychologist does not know what reasons cause prisoners suicide in prisons in general. Such as employee performance research, organizations usually do not know what reasons cause their employees' overall performance to be worse suddenly, it is possible that their families relationship is worse, or they feel wage/salary level is too low to compare the industry's average salary/wage level, or they feel their company's promotion chance is less, or they hope to change another new job. However, the organization needs to assume that poor workplace environment and/or lacking effective training course program , these both factors will cause its employees' performance to be worse suddenly. Thus, causal explanation view point, it will need to be considered to any organizations when they need to do any employee performance psychological research.

CHAPTER II

Aims and hypotheses in employee performance psychological research

The possible aims of employee psychological research is to examine research objectives as three research aspects, such as below:

1. Descriptive or exploratory studies, it concerns case studies are reports that describe a particular case in detail, for example, the case study research aim can be conceived as investigating the factors that how they can be created, to find what factors cause the consequences which can be the psychological research aim. Such as employee performance psychological research case, when the organization needs to investigate whether in general, some employee individual productive efficiency is worse, the causes are due to themselves family relationship or lacking money spending or changing new job desire etc. non –related its organizational weaknesses factors or it's organizational weaknesses factors, such as poor working environment , lacking enough facilities supply, or poor manger individual attitude, or lacking enough training to improve their efficiency. So, when the organization discover its employees perform worse suddenly. It needs to gather data to investigate whether what are the major factors to cause its employees perform worse suddenly.

2. Evaluation or outcome studies, it aims to test the effectiveness of a particular feature. This kind of research often seeks to develop theory to explain why the outcome occurrence. It simply concentrates on the consequences of certain activities without attempting to test theoretical or ideas to explain how any why the consequences are caused. For employee performance research case example, when the organization knows its employees' overall performance is worse, e.g. this month car manufacturing number is less than 50 % to compare last month . The less than 50% car manufacturing number to this month, it is the effectiveness feature. The organization expects to find the reasons why this month's car manufacturing number reduces less than 50% to compare last month suddenly. It is possible due to the machines qualities are worse and old obsolete when they are used to manufacture cars long term, needed new technologies , e.g. artificial intelligent manufacturing robots, employees feel tried to work, when they often need to overtime to work or the employees number is not enough. SO, its poor productive efficient consequence must not be caused by poor manufacturing workplace environment or lacking enough training to workers both factors. It is due to the organization itself resource shortage problem. Then, the organization needs to gather different category of data to evaluate whether why its overall employee's performance is worse to compare last month suddenly.

3. This kind of research is meta-analysis studies. It aims to summarize and analyze the results of the range of studies which have investigated a particular topic . It is in a systematic and structured way using statistical techniques. These trends may be used to calculate what is known as an effect size. This is the size of the trend in the data adjusted for the variability in the data. For employee performance psychological research example, when the organization expects to find whether the other similar competitors between owning training department and lacking training department , what are the advantages will be possible to bring or/and what are the disadvantages will be possible to bring as well as whether it has need to implement one training department to bring the possible advantages to itself. Then , it needs a systematic and structured way using statistical techniques. These trends may be used to calculate what is known as an effect size. This is the size of the trend in the data adjusted for the variability in the data for its reference sources. It aims to analyze whether the training department is needed to bring what the good or bad influences to its similar competitors in order to help itself to make the judgement whether it ought need to set up one training department or not.

What the employee performance research aim?

The employee performance researcher needs to have an understanding of what purposes the research will serve and how likely it is to serve these purposes. The employee performance researcher needs to be able to present the aims of their studies with enough clarity to justify just why the research was done in the way in which it was done. More importantly, the aims of the research need to be clearly justified by providing their rational.

In conclusion, justifying the aims research can involve: Explaining the relevance of the research to what is already known about the topic as well as reference to the wider social situation, e.g. competitors' productive efficiency and organizational development growth situation for research, employee performance psychology research is often a response to the concerns of whole society by government, social institutions, such as the legal and educational system, business organization.

What are employee psychological research hypotheses?

The use of hypotheses is more common in employee psychological performance research than in concerning , such as sociology, economics and other related subjects. A hypothesis does not have to be true since the point of research is to examine the support or its aim is for the hypothesis, e.g. One car manufacturing organization assumes that all first time new car manufacturing employees , they lack enough skills to manufacture its different kinds of cars , so it assumes that they all need to be trained to raise their car manufacturing skills to be proficient, if it expects that they can raise productive efficiency in short time, e.g. one month. It implies that it needs have one training department to provide effective car manufacturing training courses to let them to learn satisfactorily if their car manufacturing technique can be improved in short time. SO, it has both assumptions, the first is all car manufacturing workers' skills are not enough as well as the second is that an effective training courses program can improve their car manufacturing skills in short time in order to raise productive efficiency after one month.

A hypothesis does not have to be true, such as car manufacturing firm case, since the point of research is to examine the support of it's aim is for the hypothesis. So, hypotheses are assumptions to link to the aims of the study. Such as the car manufacturing firm aims to raise its car manufacturing worker's skills to be proficient after one month, so it assumes that its all new workers' skills are not proficient and it is one an effective training courses program can improve their skills to manufacture the increasing car number after one month in possible. So, it does not concern other variable factors will influence their car manufacturing performance.

However, hypotheses can contain three
variables: Attitude importance, attitude similarity, interpersonal attraction variables. These assumptions concern to research the firm's employee personal individual working attitude can be either similar, e.g. many employees' working attitude is positive or liking to work or many employees' working attitude is negative or disliking to work, or interpersonal attraction , e.g. many employees can be influenced to reduce productive efficiencies , due to the poor performance of employees' personal influence, or attitude importance in a group of student's learning behavior, such as business organization case, the team employees' overall working performance behavior can influence the other team members' working behavior obviously.So, this psychological research can assume the Classroom students' learning attitude can be either similar to hard to learn, or these students can influence interpersonal attraction to influence themselves learning attitude together in classroom or all these students' feeling which is their whole classroom's all student their learning attitudes are very important factor to influence themselves whole learning behaviors in classroom. So, such as any organizations' employees , organizations can also assume that many employee individual performance can be influenced to perform better or worse when they need to cooperate to work in different teams working environment together.

CHAPTER III

What are variables, concepts and measures meaning to any employee performance psychological research

The variable means a key concept in psychological research. A variable is anything which varies and can be measured , e.g. the organization's overall employees performance or productive efficiencies can be raised or decreased the product number in any time, it is tangible, such as manufacturing number's increasing or decreasing number. These is a distinction between a concept and how it is measured. Otherwise, hypothetical is not variable, but theoretical or conceptual inventions, which explains what we can observe in our psychological research. It is feeling and intangible.

Variables are what we create when we try to measure concepts. So, we will use the term variable without discussing the idea in any great details. Variables are the things what we measure. They are not exactly the same thing as the concepts that we use when trying to develop theories about something. For example, if one social psychological student wished to measure social influence how to influence people's behaviors in the country, the social psychological student might so, so in a number of different ways, such as number of people who disagree with a participant in s study.

The use of concepts of independent variable and dependent variables was being encouraged by experimental psychologists to replace the response. The term variable tool prominence between psychologists concludes psychological phenomena in terms of the variables familiar from statistics. In this way, psychological phenomena in terms of the variables familiar from statistics.

Dennis, H & Duncan, C. (2005, pp.39-40) indicated variables in psychology can include these sample different types: causal variable, it is only psychological domain. It is not possible to establish cause and effect sequences , simply on the basic of statistics, e.g. the organization can not find what factors cause its employees overall performance to be worse. It can only find data gathering of all similar competitors' overall worse performance analysis; hypothetical construct , it is only psychological domain, it is not really a form of variable , but an unobservable psychological structure or process , which explains observable findings, e.g. the organization assumes all new employees' overall productive efficiencies will be worse to compare the old employees and it assumes that an effective training program can improve the new employees' performance in short time; independent variable includes psychological or statistical variable in the dependent variables. As a psychological independent variable has a causal effect on the dependent variable. This is not the case when considered as a statistical concept. Ratio variable is only statistical domain, it measured on an numerical scale which has a proper new point. This allows the researcher to make ratio statements, such as person it is twice as tall as person is, such as organization's performance research, e.g. this month, this organization's manufacturing number can raise to manufacture more than three times to compare last month.

However, it is given close relationships between psychology and statistics, many variables do not readily talk into just one of these categories. This is sometimes because psychologists have taken statistical terminology and observed it into their professional vocabulary to refer to slightly different things.

It brings one interesting question concerns variable: How can a variable be the independent variable of the causal direction of the relationship between two variables is not know? E.g. When one organization believes that there is possible to cause worse performance, due to either lacking effective training or worse workplace environment, how it can prove that these two variables both can influence their employees' worse performance in the same time.

For example, variables which can be calculated number and which are characteristic of the participant , subject variables , variables can be example: How old the person is, how intelligent, they are, how anxious , they are etc. when the organization employ any one of its employees. All these variables may be described aas the independent variable by some researchers. Such as this psychological research what characteristics the participant, it can not be explained how the causal direction of the relationship between the participant's age and whether his age has relationship to cause his intelligent level, e.g. when he is younger, then he is more intelligent, so when he is older, he will be less intelligent, however, these two variables are not known by the psychological researcher. Such as the organization's employee individual age variable, which will influence their intelligent level in order to learn training courses more easily to bring effect of the raising productive efficiency in short time or the employee is younger and he is health, so the worse workplace can not influence his productive efficiency to be worse. Hence, in the organization case, it will need to try to predict what the value is of the criterion variable to the participant's psychological research from the values of the predictor variable or variables in order to decide whether what are /is the main factor(s) to influence its organizational performance.

What is quantitative variables mean?

When we measure a quantitative variable, the numbers or values we assign to each person or case represent increasing levels of the variable. These numbers are known as scores since they represent amounts of something. For example, in one quiz game to research whether whom game player is more clever, the independent variable might be age and the dependent variable may be scores on a quiz game or some other measure of general knowledge, older people do better on the general knowledge quiz game. So, age itself, is not responsible for higher scores on the quit game. Otherwise, these may be more than one variable, e.g. educational experiences to raise the quit game player's skill to earn higher scores to win any quiz game competition. So, it seems that younger age quit game player must not earn higher scores to compare the older age quiz game player.

Age factor is not the main factor . Otherwise, education all experience will prove any quiz game players' skill to raise quiz playing skill to learn how to win the quiz competition more easily. So, age and clever is not the main factor to assist quiz game player to win easily. Learning experience will be one main psychological factor to assist the quiz game player to win any quiz competition.

It concludes there is an individual effect of age to influence the quiz game players' on the scores on the quiz. Otherwise, these may be more than mediator variable , e.g. educational experiences to raise the game competition. So, it seems that younger age quiz game player must not earn higher scores to compare the older age quiz game player. Age factor is not the main factor. Such as employee psychological performance research, organizations ought assume many different factors, include the non-related organizational as well as related organizational factors in order to find whether its organization ought need to implement effective training or/and implement facility management strategy to improve workplace environment to achieve the raising productive efficiency or improving performance aim. Because each factors will be possible dependent or independent.

Reference

Dennis, H & Duncan, C. (2005), Introduction to research methods in psychology , 2 edition: New York, US Person Prentice Hall, pp. 9-10., pp. 39-40.

CHAPTER IV

Facility management can reduce maintenance service expenditure

Facility management provides a variety of non core operations and maintenance services to support any organizations' operation. For logistic organization example, it is possible to provide effective maintenance service to warehouse in order to reduce warehouse facilities to be damaged to bring to spend to buy any new equipment facilities expenditure. So, when the logistic compnay's warehouse facilities can be maintenanced to be the best quality. Then, they can be used these warehouses' machines facilities again. Their performance can assist workers to manufacture any products to keep the most efficiently an raising the best production performance in whole manufacturing process. Then, this logistic company's facility management department can bring to avoid purchase any new machine facilities expenditure spending. One to these warehouses' production machine facilities are kept in the best productin performance environment evem in long term production need.

The logistic industry's facility management department can create cost savings and efficiency of the warehouse's workplaces. It's machines facilities (producton machines) are dealt with the maintenance management of the physical assets maintenance service. FM (facilities management) has been being applied to industrial facilities in logistic and warehouse industry long term as well as maintenance plays a significant role to ensure the full service and the warehousing system, including both building components and equipment in warehouse.

Maintenance service is needed to bring a certain level of availability and reliability of a warehouse facilities system and its components and its ability perform to a standard level of quality. So , it seems that logistic industry's warehouse asset cost reducing. It depends on whether it has one facility management deparrment to provide maintenance service to itself warehouse workplace's production machine facilities and warehouse building itself in order to let workers t feel the manufacturing machines can bring good manufacturing performance to assist them to produce any products in one safe warehouse workplace environment. Hence, the performance measurement of warehouse maintenance issue will be valued to be consider to every warehouse manager and facility manager in logistic industry.

In logistic industry, (FM) works at two level on the one hand, it provides a safe and efficient working environment, which is essential to influence warehouse workers whether how they perform to do their manufacturing tasks or logistic goods delivery tasks in warehouse. When they feel the warehouse is safe environment to work. They will not need to consider anywhere has risk to cause they die by accident in warehouse. Hence, they can concentrate on doing their every tasks . On the other hand, it can involve strategic issues, such as property (warehouse workplace and management, strategy property decision and warehouse facility, e.g. manufacturing macine, facility maintenance and checking planning and maintenance planning development.

However, reducing the operating expense issue will be the main aim when the logistic company feels that it has need to set up one in-house facility management department to carry on any maintenance service for its warehouses' any workplace property and manufacturing machines facilities. So, when the logistic company decides to implement one facility management department, it needs to ensure its facility management department can bring the minimum level of keeping manufacturing performance and efficiency to its warehouses' any manufacturing machines and warehouses' property to avoid to be damaged in shourt term, such as loss of busness due to failure in service, provision of project to customer satisfaction, provision of safe environment, effective utilisation of workplace space, e.g. warehouse effectiveness and communication between the workers and the logistic managers in the warehouse workplace , due to the warehouse's space is not enough maintenance service reliability to the logistic company's warehouse, responsiveness of the warehouse's worker individual negative emotion problem, due to hs/she often feels need to work in one unsafe warehouse working environment. Hence, it seems that poor or unsafe warehouse working environment can influence workers feel negative emotion to work to bring low efficiency (inefficiency) or under productive performance in warehouse. It has relationship to influence they to bring psychological negative emotion feeling to work when the organization lacks one effective warehouse management repairing service to be provided to the warehouse's facilities and properties' maintenance needs in order to avoid ineffective measurement and misleading of performance.

Hence, the logistic company's facilities management department often needs to be reviewed whether irs maintenance service level is passed to achieve the lowest repair (maintenance) service standard to its warehouse itseld property and manufacturing machine or warehouse delivery tool facilities or warehouse lamps' light whether is enourh to let workers to see anything clearly to avoid accident occurrence or see anything to work clearly or the warehouse space areas are enough to let they can have enough space to walk or communicate to their team supervisors or deliver any goods more easily in the short distance between the worker's sending goods location and the delivering goods destination in order to avoid because the lacking enough space to cause the accident occurrence , due to the space is not enough to let they deliver their goods to any locations in warehouse.

Hence, it seems logistic company's (FM) department can contribute to the organization's mission, such as avoiding warehouse accident occurrence, inefficiency, inadequancy and unavailability of the facility for future needs when the warehouse lacks enough space areas to bring poor performance of facility and dangerous warehouse itself property in warehouse, e.g. safe and reliable operations of material handling equipment and maintenance of warehouse facilities, grounds, sesurity system, utilities, plumbing, heating , enough lightins system, air conditioning, warming heater, fire protecton, security system alarm etc. facilities in warehouse.

Hence, it seems that if the logistic company expected to reduce to spend lot of excessive manufacturing machine purchase expenditure, lossing of workers' life or bring workplace accidents , due to poor warehouse workplace environment, even bringing lawsuit compensation claim loss , due to the worker individual accident or death is caused from the poor warehouse facilities, or bring negative emotion to let the workers feel they are working in unsafe warehouse workplace environment. Then, it ought choose to set up on facility manageemtn department in order to provide enough maintenance service to its warehouse to avoid these non essential expenditure causing , due to these poor warehouse facilities factors.

Hence any logistic company ought choose to set up one itself in -house facility management department, it be better than outsourcing its all facilities service to one facility mangement (maintenance service provider) to help it to deal any kinds of maintenance service in warehouse. Because it is long term maintenace need to its warehouse's any machines and warehouse itself properties. If it chose to find one outsourcing facilitiy management maintenance service provider to replace its in-house facility mangement department to deal all related facilities maintenance tasks in warehouse. Then, it is possible that it needs to pay long time facilities maintenance service fee to its outsourcing facility management maintenance service provider more than itself facility management maintenance service provision department.

In conclusion, to decide whether the company ought need or not need facilities maintenance service or either set up in-house facility management department or outsource one facility management maintenance service provider. It depends on whether its organization has how many facilities are used in its workplace, how many staffs are working the workplace, how much size of its workplace, its workplace is office or warehouse or factory, how long time of its facilities' useful time etc. factors , then it can decide whether it needs or does not need one facility maintenance service deparment or outsouring facility maintenance service provider to help it to deal any facilities management problem in its organization.

CHAPTER V

Facility management role in organization

When one company feels that it has need facility management service. It can choose to set up either in-house facility management department or seek one outsourcing facility management service provider to help it to arrange any facility management service need. However, this facility management role is only one for the organization. It concerns this question: What facility management maintenance function can bring the benfits to the organization?

It can define that all services required for the management of building and real estate to maintain and increase their value, the means of providing maintenance support, project management and user management during the building life cycle, the integration of multi-disciplinary activities within the built environment and the mangement of their impact upon people and the workplace. In traditional, (FM) services may include building fabric maintenance, decoratin and refurbishment, plant, plumbing and drainage maintenance, air conditioning maintenance, lift and escalator maintenance , fire safety alarm and fire fighting system maintenance, minor project management. All these are hard services. Otherwise, cleaning , security, handyman services, waste disposal, recycling, pes control, grounds maintenance, internal plants. All tese are soft services. Additional services, might also include: pace planning, things moving management, business risk assessment, business continuity planning, benchmarking, space management, facilities contract outsourcing service arrangement, information systems, telephony, travel booking facility utility management, meeting room arrangement services, catering services, vehicle fleet management, printing service, postal services, archiving , concierge services, reception services, health and safety advice, environmental management.

All of these services will be every organiztion's in-house facility soft or hard services needs. So, it explains why some large organizations feel need one effective facility management department to help them to arrange how to implement facility serivices efficiently in order to achieve cost reducing, raising efficiency and performance improvemen aims because one effective facility management control system can influence employee individual productive effort to be raised or reduced indirectly.

However, (FM) can be selected either setting up one in-house (FM) department or outsourcing its services to one facility mangement service provider to help the organizatin to solve any kinds of facilities maintance service problems. One on-house (FM) department is a team, it needs employees to deliver all (FM) services. Some specialist services are needed to be outsourced, when the service is on expertise in the company. The no expertise services will be outsourced to simple service contracts, e.g. lift and escalator (FM) department will have direct labour, but it can outsource some specialist to help it to do some complect facilities management service. So, the team leader can of can manage whose team staffs, such as maintenance technicians run low risk operations . Otherwise, the outsourcing facility management service provider needs to help it to operate high risk operations or maintenance vital plant facility management service. Anyway, it can set up in-house (FM) department to arrange specialist direct labour and outsourced (FM) services to more than one facility management service providers to do different kinds of (FM) services. One of these outsourcing (FM) service provider, who can arrange sub-contractors to assist it to finish any (FM) services of it's outsourcing (FM) services are more complex to compare the other sub-contractors (third parties).

What is a facility manager's role to provide quality service to satisfy its user needs?

We need to know how quality can be defined in facility management and why it should be defined by the customer? How facility managers can find out customer (user) needs? What are the difficulties in finding out users' needs and in delivering quality services? Whether improving quality always means requiring higher cost?

In general, facility manager's major responsibilities may include these major functional areas: longer range and annual facility planning, facility financial forecasting, real estate acquisiton and/or disposal, work specification, installation and space management, architectural and engineering planning and design, new construction and/ or renovation, maintenance and operations management, maintenance and operation management, telecommunications integration, security and general administrative services. When the facility manager had implemented any one of these FM services for those user. How does he/she provide excellent (FM) service quality ot let whose users to feel satisfactory?

In fact, quality issues can not be considered without customer-oriented perspective service quality involves a comparision of expectation with performance. (FM) service quality is a measure of how well to service level delivered matches customer expectation. So, these issues are (FM) service user's general measurement level requirement. The (FM) manager needs to achieve these the minimum performance measurement level to satisfy whose (FM) user's needs.

However, (FM) service quality has three characteristics: Intangibility, heterogeneity, inseparability. But in fact, (FM) service delivered may be through tangible physical aspects, e.g. factory plant workplace building, machine equipment maintenance, intangible (FM) services, e.g. managing space moving in plant to let staffs to work, managing outsourcing cleaners to clean factory equipment. However, all (FM) service performance often varies, due to the behavior of service personnel. Hence, a well developed job specification and training can help to improve the consistence of services of (FM). Any (FM) productin and consumption of many services may are inseparable and they are ususally interactions between the (FM) client and the contact person from the service provider.

Hence, it seems that service quality is considered as hard to evaluate. In (FM) service quality, it includes physical quality and interactive non-physical service quality. Physical quality is tangibles: The appearance of the physical facilities, equipment, personnel and communication materials. Non-physical services quality means reliability: The ability to perform the promised service dependably and accurately; responsiveness means the willingness to help customers and provide promopt service to let user to feel; assurance mans the competence of the system in its credibility in providing a courteous and secure service and empathy means the approachability, ease of access and effort taken to understand customers' needs.

Hence, a good performance of (FM) manager , he/she ought satisfy the user's tangible and non-tangible both service quality needs. I recommend that he/she can attempt to predict what are the (FM) customer expects in each (FM) service needs. Then, it can make decision what aspect(s) will be the (FM) users major (FM) service need and what aspect(S) won't be the (FM) users major (FM) service need. Then, he/she can make more accurate decision to arrange time, human resource , cost spending amount arrangement whether when it ought concentrate on finishing the (FM) major service tasks as well as whether how he/she ought finish the major (FM) service tasks to be more easily, e.g. how to arrange staffs number to finish, how many the minimum staffs number is needed to be arrange the major (FM) service tasks, time arrangement is important factor, because it can influence whether he/she ought finish the major (FM) service tasks today or tomorrow or later in order to have enough time to finish other non-major (FM) service tasks. Instead of time management, staff number arrangement is also important factor , if he/she arrangeed the excessive staffs number to do the (FM) major services tasks, then it is possible that it will have shortage of staffs number to finish the non-major (FM) service tasks on the day. So, avoiding either majoe or non-major (FM) services can not finish on the day. The (FM) manager needs to predict when the major (FM) services and the non-major (FM) services which are necessary to be finished in order to have enough time and staffs to assist him/her to finish every day major and non-major (FM) servie effectively. Then, the achievement of his/her (FM) major and non-major tangible and non-tangible services , it will have more chance to be performed efficiently by his/her managed staffs.

In conclusion, in any organizations , (FM) manager needs have good predictable effort to evaluate whether when his/her managed team need to finish the major and/or non-major (FM) tasks as well as whether how he/she ought arrange the accurate time and staff number to finish any major and/or non-major (FM) service tasks on the day. Then, his/her leading of (FM) service team can be managed to work more efficiently in order to satisfy her/his (FM) service user's needs.

CHAPTER VI

How (FM) space moving management can bring valued add to organizations

There are interesting questions: How (FM) can bring value-add to avoid loss or earn more profit to the organization? Can it influence employees to raise performance and improve efficiency ? Some organizations' (FM) service need which is necessary in order to let employees can raise productivity.

It is based on these assumptions: I assume the organizations have completely either outsourced or in-house their (FM) facility management departments will gain more effect on added value than they have no (FM) function as well as organizations have a strong coordination with the (FM) department will gain more added value than organizations with a weak coordination. Organizations in the profit aim can gain more added value than organizations in the not for profit aim sectors.

In fact, any organization is difficult to confirm it has relationship between improving performance, raising efficiency and owning (FM) function in its organization. (FM) could have to do with the attraction of easy but incomplete indicators of efficiency rather than the necessarily and less direct measures if the effectiveness and the relevance of space moving useful management, e.g. whether building has the enough space to let employees to move to work easy in order to raise efficiency, whether the building has excessive furniture and equipment number and they are putted on wrong places to be caused employees move difficulty in the building in order to influence productive performance.

However, how to arrange space moving management to equipment, e.g. copying machines, faxes, productive machines, they are putted on the locations where have enough space to let employees to move to another locations. For example, the building floor has more than 50 employees, but its space is not enough to let these 50 employees to move to any locations to let them to feel easily often. Then, it is posible to cause they feel nervous pressure and they can feel difficult to work , when they are working in a small office space or factory space or warehouse space. Then, the consequence will be under-predictive efficiency or poor performance to any one of these 50 employees in this office or factory or warehouse.

" Facility management is responsible for coordinating all efforts related to planning, designing, and managing buildings and their systems, equipment, and furniture to enhance. The organizations abilty to compete successfully in a rapidly changing world." (F.Becker)

The author explains equipment, workplace internal space designing, furniture space putting location arrangement will have possible to influence employee individual productive performance or efficiency to be raised or reduced in the workplace. Hence, it seems that, in the value chain (FM) belongs to the activity part of the firm. To make the facilities cooperation with each office or factory or warehouse using space moving facility management. Facility space moving management must be linked strategically, tactically and operationally to other support activity to add value to the organization's office or factory or warehouse space moving management arrangement more effectively. Thus, how to arrangement space moving management issue it will have possible to influence the organization's employee individual productive performance and efficiency in whose workplace. It seems that (FM) space moving management arrangement have indirect relationship to influence the organization's employee individual performance and efficiency , due to they need often to work in the workplace, if they feel moving difficulty , or excessive equipment , furniture number is putting into the small office, factory or warehouse locations, or they feel the office or factory or warehouse has excessive (a lot of) staffs number to work in the small space of office or factory or warehouse. Then, they can not concentrate nervous on finishing every tasks in possible. In long term, their efficiencies will be poor or inefficiencies or their performance won't be improved or causing poort performance in possible.

Instead of the not enough space moving and excessive staffs number factor, it will bring another question: Can enough information systems equipment cause a more efficient and improved performance to the organization staffs in the workplace?

I assume that the office has 100 employees and it has only ten copying machines. So it means that ten employees use one copying machine. Hence, it brings this question: Is it enough to provide only ten copying machines to average ten employees to use? It depends on other factors, e.g. whether any one of these 100 employees needs to print how many documents per day , whether the five copying machines' locations are far away to separate different locations or they are stored in one printing room in the office, whether the day has how many staffs are absent, whether the day has how many printing machine(s) is/ are broken to need to be repaired. Hence, these unpredictable external environment factors will influence whether the five copying machines number is enough to let these 100 employees to use in the office every day. Hence, facility manager ought need to spend to observe average their copying behaviors every day in order to make data record. Many employees need to use copy machines to print documents, average how many document's page number, they need to print, how much average time spending to print their documents, average how many staff absent number on the day. Even, if the all five copying machines are stored in the printing room, calculating the staffs number whether how many staffs need more than five minutes to walk to the printing room to print their documents many staffs need to spend five minute to walk to the printing room, and they have other urgent tasks to wait to finish. It is possible to influence their efficiency, due to they often need to spend more than five minutes to walk to the printing room to print documents. If there are many staffs need to often to print documents, but their printing task will have many time, e.g. 20 separate printing tasks. Then, they need to spend at least (20x5) 100 minutes to spend time to walk to the printing room to print their documents. It must influence that they should not finish the other urgent tasks on the day. If there are many staffs to spend much time to walk to the printing room in the least 20 separate printing time or more on that day. All the facility manager needs to evaluate whether all the five copy machines are stored in the printing room whether it is the best location decision or they ought need be separated to put on different office locations in their workplaces, even he/she ought need to evaluate whether it is enough copying machines number, when the office has only 5 copying machines. He/ she ought need to buy more copying machines number to satisfy any one of these 100 employee individual copyiing task need.

In conclusion, effective office or factory or warehouse space moving facility management will be one part task of (FM) function. If the office or factory or warehouse can have accurate equipment, machine , furniture number to avoid excessive or shortage number problem to cause employees often feel moving difficult problem in their workplace when they need to move to another location to work in office or warehouse or factory as well as whether the staff needs often spend time to wait the another employee to use the copying machine to print whose document or fax machine to deliver whose document. Then, it is not that fax or printing machines number is not enough to provide the employees to use in the office or warehouse or factory workplace.

Hence, (FM) includes space moving facility management to equipment , machines, furniture number as well as choosing anywhere is(are) the suitable location (s) arrangement to putting or storing these facilities in workplace as well as decision of the staff number and the workplace area size whether it has excessive staffs number to cause these staffs need to work in the small area size of office or warehouse or factory workplace. So, the organization ought need to decide whether it needs to reduce the office's staffs number to let them to work in another more suitable locations in another workplace. Hence, all these facilities space moving management and staffs and workplace size issues will be (FM) manager's consideration issues, because these external environment factors will influence employee individual efficiency and performance to be ppor to cause low valued to its organization in long term in possible .

Reference

Becker, F. (1990). " Facility management : a cutting edge field?" property management 8 (2): 25-28.

CHAPTER VII

The relationship between facility management and productive efficiency

It is one interesting question: Can facility management function bring benefits to raise productive efficiency to organizations? I shall indicate some cases to attempt to explain this possible occurrence chance as below:

Facility management benefit to office workplace

In private organizations, when the firm has facility management department, whether it can bring efficient administration to influence clerks to work efficiently in office, e.g. reducing administrative time or shortern time to work in administrative processes, in order to achieve minimizing clerk number labor cost. How to design office facilities to let office staffs to feel comfortable to work and reducing their pressure to work. It seems that office working environment will influence office staff individual performance. If the office workin environment could improve efficiency and creativity of services to satisfy office workers' comfortable working environment needs. It will reduce every administration manager's working pressuse when he/she needs often to find methods to attempt to encourage whose administrative clerks to avoid to waste working time to do some non-major administration tasks. Hence, how to design or allocate or arrange office any facilities' stored locations or whether how many equipment number is the enough to store in the locations, which will influence office employees' working attitude in order to raise or reduce their administration tasks efficiency indirectly, e.g. the office is clean or dirty, whether office receiption has enough information telephone switchboard operation facilities, whether every clerk's table has enough computers number to supply to every to use, whether internet speed is fast or slow in order to let any employees can send and receive email to communicate or download any document from internet in short time, whether data processing and computer system maintenance service supply is enough to be repaired to employees' computers immediately when their computers are broken to wait repaire, whether website editing facilties operation whether is enough to link to office every staffs in order to let any office staffs can apply internet to do their tasks conveniently in short time.

Hence, all of these general office equipment facilities whether they are enough supplied and their stored positions anywhere are the suitable to assist any clerks to work conveniently, they will influence every office employee's administrative and productive efficiency indirectly as well as all faxs, copying machines, computers, whether internet linking maintenance service time is short or long to prepare to any office employees to use conveniently any time, these different issues will also influence every employee individual efficiency in office. Hence, it concludes that office working environment, facilities supply number, facilities maintenance service and facilities location storing both factors will influence employee individual administrative productive efficieny in office.

facility management benefits to service working environment

Can effective facility management improve service working environment to raise employee individual work performance? It is a concern about the quality of service to its customer question. The term" standards and goals" are often used to measure staff individual service performance whether he/she can serve to customers to let them to feel this staff's service performance or attitude is good or bad.

Is the service workplace working environment facilities enough, it will influence customer service staff individual performance.

For shopping center service industry case example, for this suitation, e.g. shopping center's facilities are enough or are placed to the suitable locations in order to let the shopping center's customers to feel comfortable to shopping when they enter this shopping center as well as whether the shopping center's facilities can influence the customer service staffs to serve whose shopping customers easily or difficult, due to whether the shopping center's facilities whether are adequate supplied or their locations are the best suitable positions to influence their service performance to let them to feel easier or comfortable to serve their customers in any large size shopping centers.

For example, whether the lamps' lighting energy is enough to let the shoppers to feel safe to walk to visit any shops when there are many shoppers were walking to cause crowd and they feel diffuclt to walk to avoid any body contact to any one in busy time when the shopping center has no enough lights to let them to see anywhere in the shopping center's dark environment. Then it will influence customer service staffs to feel difficult to find any shopping center customers, e.g. when two shopping center customers are fighting in one location where is far away to the shopping customer service staffs and securities in the shopping center, because the shopping center is large and it has no enough light to let the customer service staffs and securities to find their frighting location to deal their fighing behavior and other shopping center's shoppers will feel very dangerous to walk their fighting location to avoid to close them. Then, it will has possible to cause death or hurt to any one of these two fighting shoppers ,even other shoppers' lifes. Because the shopping center's securities and customer service staffs who need to spend much time to find their fighting location, it will delay they can bring the policemen to their fighting location when they arrive this shopping center's destination in short time in order to solve their fighting behavior to influence all shoppers' lifes in this shopping center. Hence, the shopping center whether it has enough lamps number and the lamps' light whether is enough, these lighting facilities will influence any shopping center customer service staffs and securities who can spend less time to arrive any locations to deal any urgent matters.

For another suitation in shopping center, if the shopping center has no enough paying telephone service facilities to supply shoppers to phone to anyone when they feel need to phone to any in the shopping center. Then, it will lead to some shoppers decide to find where the shopping center's receiption's telephone to supply to them to phone call to anyone. If ther are ten shoppers are waiting to use the shopping center's receiption's telephone to phone call to their friend or family within one minute. Thus, it will influence the reception customer service staffs feel difficult to arrange how to distribute the only one telephone to these ten shoppers to use to phone call their friend or family when they are queuing within their one minute waiting time in the shopping center's reception. If these ten shoppers can not use the receiption telephone to phone call anyone. hen, they will feel disatisfactory and complain to the reception service staffs unpolitely. So, lacking enough facilities in the shopping center's any where, it will possible to influence their shopping centers' shoppers to feel all shopping center's service staff individual performance to be poor. It means that if the shopping center expects to improve customer satisfaction to its customer service staff's behavioral performance, it meets have enough facilities to be supplied in the shopping center to let its shoppers to feel it is one comfortable and safe shopping center. In conclusion, shopping center's facilities will have possible to influence shoppers' feeling to evaluate its customer service staffs to evaluate whether their service attitudes are good or poor indirectly.

Can facility management improve productivity

The productivity means resources (input) is therefore the amount of products or services (output), which is produced by them. Hence, higher (improved) productivity means that more is produced with the same expectton of resource, i.e. at the same cost is terms of land materials, machine, time or labor. Alternatively, it means same amount is produced at less labor cost in term sof land, material, machine, time for labor that is utilized. So, it brings this question: How can facility management improve productivity? I shall explain as these several aspects, it is possible to be improved productivity from (FM) successfully.

Improved productivity of farm land: If the farming land has better facility management to bring advantages by using better seed, better facilities of cultivation and most fertilizer. It is in the agricultural sense is increased (improved). So, facility management can bring benefits to any land resource to raise productivity in possible. It implies that the productivity of land used for better facility management of industrial purposes is said to have been increased if the output of products or service within that area of industrial land is increased output aim.

Improved productivity of material: If the factory has improved better equipment by facility management method to assist skillful workers to raise the manufacture cloth number, then the productivity of the cloth number is improved by (FM) method.

Improved productivity of labour: When the factory has good manufacturing equipment facilities to be supplied to improve methods of work to product more producing number per hour, then (FM) improved productivity of worker. Hence, in any workplaces, when organization has good facilities, it will influence employees to raise productivities in possible, because they need often to improved equipment facilties manufacture products to achieve higher producton number aim.

Can facility management raise bank employee
productivity

Bank workplace environment is busy, the bank counter service staffs need to contact many bank clients to help them to serve or withdraw money from bank's counters. Whether does the quality of environment in bank workpace will influence the determination level of employee's motivation, subsequent performance productivity in bank working environment. For example, if the bnk's staffs need work under inconvenient conditions , it will bring low performance and face occupatinal health diseases causing high abenteeism and turnover.

In general, bank size is usually small, it will have many bank clients enter bank to contact counter staffs to need them to help them to save or withdraw money. So, it will bring air pollution the crowd queue in every bank counter challenge when the bank has many people are queue waiting in counters to queue. So, bank working condition problem relates to environmental and physical factors which will influence every bank counter staff individual working performance to serve bank clients satisfactory. However, bank staffs need to deal many documents concern every client personal data every day. So, they need to spend much time to use computer and painting machines. This is particularly true for these employees who spend most of the day operating a computer terminal in bank workplace. As more and more computers are being installed in workplaces, an increasing number of business has been adopting designs for bank offices installment. So, bank needs have effective facilities management design because of demand of bank staffs for more human comfort.

An good equipment facility management for bank staffs to use conveniently, it is assumed that better workplace environment can motives bank employees and produces better productivity. Hence, bank office environment can be described in terms of physical and behavioral components to influence bank staffs to work inefficiently. To achieve high level of abnk employee productivity, bank organizations must ensure that the physical environment in conductive to bank different department organizational needs, facilitating interaction and privacy, formality and informality, functionalit and disciplinarily, e.g. house loan or private loan departmets, counter service department, visa card application department.

Thus, in a high safe privary facility management working environment will let different department bank staffs feel safe to worry about privacy loss in possible. So, the improving bank facility to bring safe and high privacy to avoid bank client individual loss in working environment issue, the facility management can be results to bring these benefits, such as in a reduction in a number of complaints and absenteeism and an increase in productivity.

Can (FM) create value to organization?

(FM) can reduce managing facilties as a strategic resource to add value to the organization and its overall performance, e.g. saving the energy in building and take care of shuttle buses and parking facilities space management for brikes, on economic efficiency and effectiveness, or good price and value for the organization.

If the organization expects to apply (FM) process to save energy, it depends on possible input factors, i.e. interventions in the accommodation facilities services. So, it seems that the organization expects to save its energy consumption in its building. It needs have goos space management facilities between parking its shuttle buses and brikes in its property's car park.

Why does space facility management is important to influence efficiency and productivity. For one school's building example, when the school decides none of the two gymnasiums student sport entertainment centers to be built in order to reduce financial cost and higher benefits. Remarkably, the use of space with the school overall strategic goals , such as creating spaces that better can support the teaching, motivate students and teachers, attract more students and increase the utilisation of existing space to accomodate an increasing number of students.

If it hopes to make high quality teaching facilities on student's choice where to study. The school will need to choose to build either one comfortable and new design facility teaching accommodation or build two gymnasium sport entertainment centers in its limited land space either for students' learning or sport aim. Due to it feels new teaching accommodcation can make more attractive to increase students numbers to choose it to study more than building

two new gymnasusm sport centers to let them do sport in school.
Hence, space choise (FC) management strategy will be one important considerable issue, when the organization has limited land space resources to make choose to build any constructions in order to increase many clients number. Such as the school organization has limited stortage land resource to let it to build either two gymnasium sport entertainment centers or one new teaching accommodation in order to attract many students to choose it to learn. Hence, it needs to gather data to make more accurate evaluation to decide how to apply its space facility to choose to build these both kinds of buildings in order to achieve the attractive student learning choice aim, so whether teh two sport entertainment activity centers or one new teaching accommodation choice, it needs to gater information to decide whether the school ought to choose to build which kind of building in order to achieve the increase of student number aim, so space facility management will be this school's land shortage problem.

CHAPTER VIII

The relationship between facility management and consumer behavior

How and why shop facility management can influence consumer individual shopping behavior? If it is possible, what shop facility management factors can influence their consumption decision when they enter the shop to plan to buy anything. I shall indicate some shop case studied to expline whether how and why every shop's facility management can influence consumer individual consumption desire when any one consumer enters any shops.

Shop's low ceiling height location (FM) influcence consumer behavior

Can the shop's ceiling height influence shoppers' shopping behavior? Can the shops's variation in ceiling height can influence how consumers process information to decide to make purchase decision in the shops, e.g. for this suitation, when the consumer enters the shop, he/she feels the ceiling height is low and it has a lamp wil contact his/her head in possible. So, he/she chooses to move far away from the low ceiling beight location in the shop. It is possible that shop's ceiling low height and the lamp locates at the ceiling low height position will influence many customers' choices to leave the low ceiling height and lamp location, then the shop's low ceiling height will have possible to influenced many customers to choose to find the another shop to buy the similar kind of products , due to the lamp locates in the low ceiling height, so this lamp and low ceiling height will be possible factor to influence any shoppers who won't choose to walk to this dangerous location in the shop. If the shop's all spaces are ceiling height and it has many lamps are located at the low ceiling height spaces. Then, it will be serious to cause many shoppers do not want to spend too much time to choose any products in the shop because they feel dangerous to walk to the any low ceiling height lamps' locations in the shop.

Hence, hoe to design the different concept may be activated by the showroom ceiling if it were relatively high, as it tends to be in mall stores, versus low, as it is in most strip mall shops and outlet centers. Relatively high ceilings may bring safe shopping emotion to let any consumers to feel thoughts related to freedom, whereas lower ceilings may let consumers to feel dangerous to walk the locations in any shops. Hence it seems any shops ought not neglect whether their ceiling height is tall and the lamps ought avoid to locate in any low ceiling height locations in order to influence consumers number to be decreased.

Can house facility management influence consumer individual purchase intention?

When one new property is built, whether the property consumers will consider how the new property is facilited to influence their purchase intention to the property will the new property's (FM) influence buyers in real estate markets' preferences choice and living interest. Any new property's internal characteristics of the house unit itsel , such as rooms available, when example, of external are location, accessibility to utilities services and facilities will have possible to influence the property buyer's final property purchase decision, so it seems that even the property price is cheap, it is not represent the property buyer will choose to buy the property, if he/she feels the property's facility mangement is poorer to compare other similar kinds of properties.

So, it can help real estate analysts better explain and predict the behavior of decision makers in real estate markets. Property consumers will search for property information, concerns the property's quality, price distinctiveness, ability, facility mangement, service of the property's external environment to decide whether the property is high value to choose to buy to compare other kinds of properties.

However, the external environmental forces, such as limited resources, e.g. time or financial will influence whose property consumption choice and living the property's satisfaction feeling (represent) a feedback machanism from post-property purchase reflection used to inform subsequent decisions. The process of the property buyer's leaving experience will serve to influence the extent to which the property consumer how to consider future next time property purchases decision and new information methods. Hence, when one property consumer chooses to buy a house, it refers house features ar house internal attributes , such as quality of building, the design as well as internal and external design, which are important factors for a property consumer when he/she needs to select and purchases one house.

The other (FM) factors which can influence the property consumers' needs, include living space as features, such as the size of kitchen, bathroom, bedroom, living bath and other rooms available in the house. The environment of housing area is also important factor, e.g. the condition of the neighbourhood, attractiveness of the area, quality of neighbouring houses, type of neighbouring houses, type of neighbouring houses, density of housing, wooded area or free coverage, slope of the attractive views, open space, non-residential uses in the areas vacant sites, traffic noise, level of owner-occupation in neighbourhoos, level of education in neighbourhood level of income in neighbourhood, security from crime, quality of schools, religious of neighbourhood, transportation , shopping center, sport entertainment can be supplied to close to the house area. All these human related issue of the property's location will also influence the property buyer's living location selection. Hence, above (FM) influence property consumer purchase behavior, it is based on the relationship behavior. The consumer's house purchase intention and house features, living space, environment and distance to recreation center, supermarket, library etc. public facilities variable (FM) factors.

In conclusion, the house internal space facility management and external environment facility management factors will influence property consumer individual house purchase intention.

The effects of in-store shelf design facility management factor influences consumer behavior

Can every store retailer's shelf design influence supermarket and large retail stores shoppers' behaviors when they visit the stores? However, currently many stores tend to build on traditional and repetitive design for their store shelf layout, it brings results in outdated store layouts.

Another important store shelf layout design aspect, retailer should consider carefully is the allocation of products on shelves. So, it seems that efficienct shelf space allocation management does not only minimize the economic threats of empty product shelves, it can also lead to higher consumer satisfaction, a better customer relationship.

Why does supermarket shelves design is important? Any retail tore will sell product category within a shelf. They can use the same nominal category , e.g. negular crisps next to light crisps, same food prouct shelf. Anyway, a goal-based shelf display can contain several product, that determine a common consumer goal, e.g. fair trade. Hence, these two categorical product structuring methods are also described in terms of how to put product, or food on shelf benefit and attribute -based product categories.

These shelf design food or product storing method will have more influence consumers to choose to buy the supermarket or retail store food or products more easily , due to products, or food put on their shelf very convenient and systematic to attract consumers' shopping consideration to the supemarket or retail store.

Music (FM) environment influence consumer consumption desire

Is it possible that shop music (FM) environment can raise consumer purchase desire? In one shop or supermarket, it can provide soft music (FM) equipment to let consumers can listen soft music or songs in the supermarket or retail shop when the are staying to spend more time shopping and whether soft music facility can be expected to raise customer individual value-added options to the music facility shop in the supermarket ot retail shop.

Can the music facilities prolong consumers to stay in the store? It is possible that tempo soft music can influence consumers to stay longer time in restaurants and supermarkets and retail shops. It is possible that the different types of music (FM) in any supemarket, restaurant, retail shop owning music listening facility shopping environment. It will have possible to influence consumers to prolong staying in their shops. For example, one wine selling retail shop has classical music (FM) listening equipment to let consumers to listen when they enter the wine shop, it is possible to cause consumers to choose to buy more expensive wine products. Some researchers indicate when the wine shop owns classical music facility to let all consumers can list classical music when they walk in the wine ship, it can evoke the wine consumers to choose to buy purchasing higher prices wine products in the long term classical music listening environment. Otherwise, in a fitness sport center, musical fir and excite or popular music (FM) environment can attract fitness sport players' emotion to play and kind of fitness sport facility longer time. Also, in one supermarket, the soft music facilities listening environment can persuade or attract food consumers to spend more time in the mall consuming food or beverage also purchase othe products more easily, due to they will listen soft music to be influenced to choose to prolong staying time in the supermarket. It seems that it has relationship between retail shop's music facility environment and consumer's emotion will be influenced by these different kinds

of soft music or songs to raise consumption desire in the supermarket, if some consumers like to proplong to stay longer consuming time in the owning music facility environment's retail shop.
In fact, some researchers indicate the owning background music facility selling environment's ship , it can affect consumer decision making, memory, concentration consumption desire. So, classical , jazz soft music facility ought be installed in restaurants, retail shops, restaurants' environment. Otherwise, popular , exciting, noise, pop music facilty ought be installed in fitness sport centers, theme park entertainment parks business places in order to influence fitness sport players or theme park entertainers to prolong playing or entertaining time to feel real sport or entertainment theme park playing machine facility's entertainment enjoyable feeling as well as attracting restaurant or supermarket or retail shop's consumers to proplong their staying time to make consumption decisions. Hence, it seems that music facility environment can raise consumers' consumption desire in possible.

University bookstore atmospheric factors how to influence student's purchase book behavior?

Any university bookstore how to do international control and structuring of book internal environment to raise students' purchase book desires in university itself school's bookstore, it will be one popular question to any universities. Hence, whether the university bookstore internal (FM) factors include: lighting, music, colors, scents, temperature, layout and general cleanliness as well as university external factors include: the university bookstore shape/size, windows, university parking facility for students availability and location,which can play an influential role of the university bookstore image in order to influence the university itself students to choose to buy books from themselves bookstore or university outside bookstores.
Whether the university student needs to spend how long individual learning time and how mcuh learning nervous to spend time to choose any kinds of book in the univeristy bookstore or outside bookstores, this issue , he/she will consider. Because he/she does want to expect spend much time and nervous to choose to buy books in any bookstore. If the universitt's bookstore physical location and internal (FM) desing image can let its target student customers to feel it's all book products are stored in any attractive internal book shelves places, e.g. the cheapest and the most expensive different subjects of text books are stored in one system method to bring the positive image of value snd quality in order to let university target student customers can find their books' choice location to spend less time to search any books to read in the unviersity bookstore easily.
However, due to learning time is shortage to every university student of the universty's book shelves can display all text books in the attractive right locations in the university bookstore as well as the university's bookstore ought has an adequate space to let university students to walk to anywhere and find any subjects of text books and compare their book sale prices in the bookstore's any shelves' locations easily when they walk to the subject of book shelf location, then they can make accurate decision either to buy the right kind of subject book or not buy it to read in the short time. They will ferl their book choice purchase decision making process won't influence their learning time in themselves univeristy. Then, the university students will be influenced by themselve university's bookstore's attractive external university facilites in the univeristy's any teaching places and the university's bookstore internal attractive environment facility image which can influence the students to make final choices to buy their liking books to read from their university's itself bookstore. Hence, the university's bookstore internal and external building environment (FM) design factors will influence its students whether choose to buy from themselves bookstore or another outside general bookstore.

How and why does retail atmospheric environment influence consumers behavior in retail shop?

Any shop's internal facility management design can influence atmospheric environment to influence consumer individual shopping desire, e.g. colour, lighting, music, crowding, design and layout factors, which internal shop (FM) environment can influence the first time shopping visiting client ' cognitive process how to feel the shop store image. Such as if the store's (FM) environment can bring enjoyable and fun and happy image to let them to feel shopping's enjoyment.
In conclusion, when consumers will like to stay longer time in the store. Due to the store's internal (FM) atmospheric environment can attract them to stay longer time in the store. Then, the customer's shopping value will raise and it can bring purchasing intention and shopping satisfaction. How can (FM) influence retail atmospheric physical (FM)

environment ? Can (FM) bring indirect relationship to influence how the consumer individual causes positive or negative purchase intention when he/she has influence to proplong staying desire in the store, when the shop has good (FM) , it will bring long time to make consumption chance in the shop.

CHAPTER IX

Facility management influences consumer satisfactory service level

Can facility management (FM) quality influence consumer satisfactory service feeling? Any organization's facility management can improve the effectiveness of the maintenance organization. It can provide improved operational and maintenance functions to maintain the physical environment to support the overall mission. However, any organization will consider whether it improves its facilities, it will raise consumer satisfactory feeling when it provides the service to them, e.g. education service industry, when students need to often to attend any school's classrooms or lecture halls, computer rooms, libraries, all these facilities will be student;s learning environment. If these school facilities can be maintenanced to let students to feel comfortable to enjoy to study in their schools' any learning locations. Then, it has possible that to bring their enjoyable learning feeling in theirs schools.

How school's facility management influences student's learning satisfactory feeling.

However, in education industry case, the school's facility management has those criteria can be used to meaure effectiveness. Student individual response time between the student's request for computer use service in school computer rooms, library reading service in school library , classroom computer facilities and tables, chairs etc. furniture supplies service and the facility managment supply number and available to useful time. If the student believes that the response time is too long when he/she feels need to use any school facilities, the actual number of seconds or minutes, he/she needs to wait how long time to queue to use his/her school's any facilities in library, classroom, computer room. So, the student's queus waiting time to use any his/hser school's facilities, it can measure the school's facility managment effectiveness.

Scheduling of preventive maintenance activities.

It schedules of any maintenance activities are not arranged effectively to the school. Then, it will influence students' poor learning facility service to their school. For their situation, when the school's first floor has two men toilets are damaged. They are needed to be required. However, it is one week period, the first floor 100 students can not use the first flooe men toilets. Hence, in this week, all 100 students need to go to other floors toilets to often use. They will feel busy and time is not enough when they need to attend to any classrooms to listen the first floor classrooms teachers' lesson. If he/she arrives the first floor classroom too late, due to he/she needs to go to another floor male toilets to queue to use. Then, he/she will feel angry and worries about whose absent or late attending classroom behavior when the lesson's teacher has attended early in the first floor clasroom , and he teacher will need him/her to explain why he/she will go to this classroom lately, if his/her explanation won't be accepted to attend to the first floor classroom too late in the week. So, arrangement maintenance schedule to any school's facilities issue is importnt to influence student's satisfactory feeling to the school. Also, lacking of preventive maintenance activities will bring results in unscheduled shutdown of critical equipment can have an unrecoverable impact on the school's good learning environment providing to student's mission.

In fact, however in any organizations, such as school, ship, office etc. organizations, achieving balance of effectiveness and efficient difficulties and takes time and effort on the part of management and staff. It is not enough to establish an optimal relationship between these two parts. It has another factor that organizations need to consider costs. In today's budget tightening environment, decreasing expenses requires accepting a lower level of efficiency and effectiveness. The goal is to determine the point at which decreasing efficiency and effectiveness is no longer acceptable before that point is reached.

It brings this question : How to apply facility managment knowledge to rise efficiency and effectiveness in order to improve quality standard of service to satisfy consumers' needs in short time? Such as school's facilities service case. What factors can influence student's level of satisfaction with regards to higher educational facilities services? It seems that any school's facilities will influence its students how to satisfy its education service indirectly. Because they need often to go to school to learn. So, any school's facilities, e.g. classrooms, computer rooms, libraries, toilets, lecture halls, canteens, sport and entertainment centers, research laboratories, school car parks, student enquiry counters, all these places to the school's any students will attend. So, how raise schools' facilities improvement to satisfy students' learning needs in the school's any locations which will have help to influence it student individual satisfaction level to the school's service, instead of every teacher individual teaching performance service to the school's students.

For any service organizations , such as hotels, restaurent, financial institutions, retail stores and hospitals etc. The physcial environment can influence how customers' evaluation of their service. Due to service has intangible nature, so customers will rely on evaluate service quality.

Any higher education institutions are education service providing organizations. They need have comfortable and enjoyable educational environment to be provided to the students to attend the school's any places in order to meet whose learning expectations and studying experience needs. So, the school's facility management will be one factor to influence student's learning satisfaction when they expect to attend the school's any locations or places to let them to feel the school's learning environment have good facility management feeling.

In fact, if the school has comfortable classrooms or lecture halls educational environment to let its students to feel, it will bring assistance to raise their learning satisfactory feeling. So, comfortable learning facility management environment is one kind of school's facility service characteristics, it includes intangibility, perishability, inseparability and variability. So, they are every student individual learning feeling when they are attending to the school's any learning locations. So, school's facility management service feeling will influence whether they expect to choose this school to study. If the school's facility management learning environment is more comfortable and teaching facilities are better to compare other schools' facilities. Then, it will have possible to attract many students to choose this school to study. Such as any educational organizations, instead of the teachers (lecturers and professors) whose educational level is influence students number. The university's building environment will inlfuence students' learning feeling, when they attend in the university. The facilities include laboratories, lecture theatres an offices, but also residential accommodations, catering facilities, sports and recreations cemtres because university students need have univesity life feeling to let them to fell the university can give welfare services , e.g. medical services, career guidance, sport entertainment, residential accommodation etc. service, instead of educational learning service in classrooms and lecture theatres. Hence, university's diversification facilities services are needed to satisfy university students to choose it to study, instead of university teacher's educational performance.

When one student can enrol the university to study from secondary education institution. The admitted student will usually consider two aspects to decide to choose the university to study. One aspect is the academic programs, of sequence of courses choices and the another aspect is the university's facilities whether they can satisfy their universoty life need, e.g. library, dorms, bookstore, food canteen , gym's sport entertainment, education technological facilities in the classrooms and lecture theatres to let the students to feel the university's teaching facilities are achieved his/her learning demand.

So, these two factors (teaching and learning and facilities) are linked to each other to influence student's total school learning experience and attitude towards a particular institution and this is termed as value chain in the student's learning process in the university. Hence, student individual evaluation variables will include teaching staff, teaching method, enrolment and facility enough supply actual service need.

However, the university's facilities, such as any residential accommodation, canteen, library , classroom, lecture theatre, sport gym, entertainment center will be their useful facilities need to satisfy their learning, entertainment and eating ,even living need in residential accommodaton in the school's learning life experience every day. If one student chooses to live in the university residential accommodation . All of his/her learning and eating and living time and spending will be calculated to the university's any facilities to let him/her to feel it can provide enough facilities to let him/her to enjoy.

Hence, the facility management factor, such as overall campus environment, library, laboratory, classroom, lecturer theatre size and facility supply of on campus accommodation, welfare right service, parking areas, cafeteria , sport center etc. They will be every studetn;s facilities service needs from the university supplies choice. So, any university ought not reglect how to improve itself university's space area facilities to achieve satisfy their needs after they choose this universoty to study. Hence, any university's facility management will influence how the studetn's satisfactory learning service feeling when he/she chooses the university to study.

In conclusion, better facility management will attract more students to choose the university to study. Otherwise, worse facility management will not attract more students to choose to study the school. Hence, it seems that the school's facility managment factor has relationship to influence student's satisfactory feeling, instead of teacher individual teaching performance factor to the school.

Property facility management influences householder buying behavior

One new property's low price is attractive factor to influence property buyer individual preference choice. Does the new individual's facility management factor influence the property buyer's preference choice decision, if the property buyer feels its facility management is better than other similar properties, even it's price is higher thn other properties. I shall indicate some cases to analyze this possibility as below:

Some properties' facility management service quality has possible to create true value for any property buyers when they consider the calculation ingedients to make decision whether to new property has higher value to choose to buy. The factors may include: price, natural environment, transportation tools convenient available, shopping centers supplies, the neighbour quality, and the property's internal facility management etc. factors.

In fact, car or house purchase buyers, they have similar behaviors. It is that car's buyers will consider the car's machines whether they are safe to drive on roads, instead price, manufacture loyalty factors. It is possible that the car's machines quality factor will be preference to any car buyers when they make preference decisions to choose which brand its cars are the suitable. However, if the car's brand is famous and its appearance beautiful and price is cheap. But the car consumer feels its machine qualities are unsafe to let the driver to drive on road. Then, the car's poor machine quality factor will influence the car buyer's decisions to choose to buy this car. It can influence the car buyer individual car purchase decision.

The car buyer's behavior is similar to property buyer's behavior. Although, the new property price is cheap, good neighbours are living near to the new property's location, shopping centers and transportation tools are available to near to this new property's area. But if the property buyers' feels its facility management is poor quality to compare other similar properties. Then, the poor quality of facility management factor will have possible to influence the property buyers whose final buying decision to choose to buy this new property. It brings this question: How and why can the facility management poor quality factor influence property consumers' preference choice?

In general, all property consumers won't know whether the new property's facility management is good or bad quality , they need to spend time to visit to the new property in order to observe whether its internal facility is satisfactory to his/her acceptable lèvel. In simple, their purchase decision will regard to how to allocate household budget, how the household's economic resources are influenced, e.g. for travelling, visits to restaurants, comparing the different similar types of property product groups, e.g. apartments or houses or houses of a givn size data. For example, if one property's room(s) size is (re) small to compare other kind similar product type of room(s) size. Although the prior property's price is cheaper to compare to the later properties. But, if some property buyers hoped the property has large room(s) size, then the later larger room(s) size which will be possible to some property buyer's preference choice. Even, their property price is more expensive to compare the smaller room(s) size of properties. Thus, the property's room size which will be one major factor to influence property buyers' purchase decision. room's size had relationship to facility management issue. Morevoer, if the room's quality and design is attractive, then it will bring more attractive to persuade some property buyers to choose to buy them to live in preference.

Hence, whether the new property is good durable product feeling which will influence householder's choice. If the householder feels the new property has long term durable life to avoid to spend much maintenance expense when they have been living in the new property for a long term period. They will believe it has better facility management, quality to let them to live longer time and the most importance is that they do not need to spend any maintenance expense , due to the property 's any internal facilities are damaged easily.

The external factors may include: culture, reference groups, faily, social class and demography of lifestyle as well as internal factors may include: feelings, past property buying and living experience , property knowledge, motivation of the property buyer individual psychology. These both factors can influence any property buyer individual decision making process to do final house purchase behavior. However, internal factors, such as: property knowledge of facility management and property living experience, e.g. how to evaluate to choose to buy the property , due to the property buyer's past living experience for the past property's facilities whether its facilities can satisfy its property buyers' comfortable living needs. This internal factor will be more important to influence any property buyer's property purchase final decision. If he/she feels whose prior old property's facilities are satisfactory. Then, he/she will compare this new property and old property's facilities to decide whether this new property is value to buy. So, the old property's facility will be the measurement standard to compare his/her next new property purchase choice. So, the property purchaser will compare these new and old property's property facilities product knowledge to similarities among property alternative which will influence his/her final decision to choose to buy the new property to live.

It seems that property low price factor must not guarantee to attractive many property buyers' choice. Otherwise, it is assumed that many property buyers like rent or buy to live the property for themselves for long term intention. There are less property buyers expect to sell the first property to earn profit intention. So, they will usually consider whether the property is long term durable product to avoid to pay maintenance expense when they had been living in the property in long term.

Some factors that taking consideration are proximity to the specific location, housing prices, developer's brand, the payment scheme, reference group, which are not the main factors to influence any property buyer individual choice. Because property buyer's need is that the property has good facilities to supply to them to live, e.g. good heater equipment can provide hot water to them to bath in winter or good air conditioners can provide cold temperature to let them to feel cool comfortable feeling in summer in their homes. Good electric tools facilities , when they have need to use electricity in safe environment at home, e.g. car park accessibility facility , level of security facility , surface areafacility and housing types, bedroom, bathroom facilities, quality of housing manufacturing raw material, house design , house durable guarantee, speed of complaint responsiveness, specification accuracy, confirmation of building plan service, showing legal file property purchase process service, finance instalments process assistance, speed of responsiveness, officers' skills of presentation. All of above these concern property facility management issues will influence any property buyers' final choice to decide whether the property is value to buy. So, facility management will influence property purchaser individual final decision in possible.

Hotel facilities influence hotel consumer choice

Travellers choose hotel to live. They will consider price, room comfortable feeling, hotel location , gum sport or entertainment service facility supplies , hotel room booking service etc. factors to decide whether the hotel can achieve every traveller individual minimum living need. However, whether hotel facilities factor will be the main factor to influence travellers' living needs. How and why do travellers consider hotel facilities whether are enough supply or facilities of quality to satisfy their demand to cause their living choice to the hotel final decision.

Usually, hotel's customers won't plan to live too long time, e.g. more than three months in the hotel. Because they are travelling aim. It will bring this question: Does hotel facilities quality consider to influence their hotel living choice if the traveller is short-term traveller to the country? However , some travellers who have effort to spend money to live high class hotels, even their journey is short trip. Hence it seems that short trip , hotel living reason can not influence the high class hotel travellers' living comfortable demand to the high class hotel room. Hence , the high class hotel room's facility management quality is also needed high performance. Even, when they need to eat breakfast, luch , dinner in the high class hotel canteens or playing any sport equipment, or gum equipment or wathcing movie in the hotel's small cinema room . They must need high class hotel can supply more entertainment, restaurant , sport facilities to satisfy their comfortable needs in the high class hotel. Moreover, they must consider safety issue when they are living in the high class hotel. So, thy must demand the hotel have enough five frighting equipment equipment in their rooms, or corridors and the stairs to let them can leave the dangerous locations to arrive the most safe locatons immediately when the hotel has fire accident occurrence in any where . So, it ensures that the high class hotel's customers must ensure the high class hotel's facilities can satisfy their any one of above these needs before they decide to live this high class hotel.

In fact, high class hotel's room price must be more expensive to compare the low class hotel. So, it explains why high class hotel's consumers will need the hotel has safe and good quality of facilities to let them to feel it is one reasonable price, safe , good service and good facilities' high class hotel to live. Usually, when the traveller arrives the country to travel, the travelers chooses the hotel to live, it is whose first time visit in common. So, he/she ought consider that the hotel environment seems it is good or bad to let the traveller to select to live. If the hotel's facility environment is new and beauty and design colorful to let the first time travellers to feel. Then, it is possible that good facilities environment can influence the first time travellers to select to live, even the hotel's room price is more expensive to compare other similar hotels in the travelling living places. Hence, it explains why hotel facilities can influence traveller individual room booking choice. When he/she is the first time to visit the hotel to select whether to live or not.

How and why facility management can influence workplace productivity to bring customer satisfaction

Facility management is one part of manufacturers or retailers as their productivity in workplace as their input and functionalistics within physical environment. In fact, facility management in workplace may include: site selection, property disposal, site acquisition, workplace space allocation, space inventory, space forecasting facility mangement, interior furniture change planning, interior furniture installation, moving maintenance, inventory, design evaluation, employment satisfaction evaluation plan, external maintenance and breakdown maintenance, preventive maintenance, landscape maintenance, energy space facility management, hazardous waste disposal, capital , operating furniture budgeting. So, it seems that one workplace considered whether the workplace's facility is enough to let employees to work in order to raise efficiency and improve productive performance more easily. Then, it will bring this question:

How and why workplace facility management can influence consumer individual satisfaction?

Strategic FM delivery is essential for business survival. I shall explain why for delivery is important to influence customer satisfaction. In business process vire point, an effective and meaningful service to their customer , i.e. the user. For logistic industry, the product's delivery time will influence when the product can be sent to the user's arrival destination. If the product is delayed to sent to the user's home or office or any location destination. The reason is because the logistic product sender has no efficient facility management (FM) arrangement in its warehouse . Then, its warehouse lacks efficient (FM), which will cause users to feel its delivery service is poor and they will complain its delivery service staffs. Then, they will find another delivery service company to replace its service. So, it explains that logistic industry's warehouse (FM) service arrangement can raise efficient time to send any products to their customers in order to let they feel satisfactory service. For example, Amazon online logistic company's warehouse has applied artificial intelligence robotic tools to assist warehouse workers to arrange the different kinds of products to deliver to the right shelves . Then, the warehouse robotics will follow their right product shelves locations to follow the right products to deliver to US domestic or overseas product buyers in the short time and it can avoid the wrong products to deliver to the wrong buyers' risk. Also, the (AI) delivery tools can raise thime efficiency to assist Amazon warehouse workers to reduce their work load, and tried to work in large warehouse environment. Although, its warehouse's area is large, the (AI) tools facility can help them to deliver the different products to different shelves in the right locations , e.g. exact product number and the kinds of product to be delivered to the right country' client's shelf location in the warehouse. Also, it imilies FM is very important to influence Amazon warehouse delivery efficiency and avoiding delivery wrong occurrence chance. For example, the shelf location belongs to US domestic customers, or the shelf location belongs to Japan customers, or the shelf location belongs to Hong Kong customers, or any other Asia or Western countries' different customers' locations. The waerhouse's facility needs have different countries' shelves enough space to put and it also need enough space to let the (AI) tools, robotic delivery workers and human workers both to walk to different shelves locations easily and the different countries' shelves number needs to be calculated accurate. For example, it has how many client number will buy Amazon's the kind product per day. If it has above 5,000 to 10,000 China clients to buy the kind of product. Then, it will need to make judgement how many shelves are placed in the warehouse. So, it can avoid to lack enough shelves to put any different kinds of products to prepare to delviery to China clients in efficienct time and it won't avoid to delay to deliver to their homes or offices or any locations in China.

Hence, such as Amazon logistic case, it explains why warehouse's space shelves number and area or locations facility management can influence workers or (AI) delvery tools how to move convenietnly and avoding the delviery to the customer's wrong destination chance occurrence and shortening time to deliver products to its clients efficienctly. Then, due to the delivering time is shorten and the wrong delivery destination's occurrence chance is also reduced , even it can avodi to deliver the product to wrong client's destination occurrence. Then, the logistic firm's clients will feel more satisfactory to its product sale delivery service and their complaints will be avoided. Hence, it explains effective warehouse (FM) space management service arrangement is essential to any logistic businesses nowadays.

Facility management brings departmental benefits

Why do organizations need have facility management (FM) service? As above examples indicate that (FM) can improve workplace environment facilities, e.g. warehouse environmet to let workers to raise efficiencies or improve performances, even it can influence consumers to raise satisfactory to it's services indirectly, also it can help organizations' equipment to be used long term to cause old and are needed to spend expenditure to maintenance or change new equipment in order to improve better quality . So , it can assist organizations to avoid to spend more expenditure for new equipment purchase or maintenance. All these issues will be facility management service's benefits to an organizations, which can concern raising customers' service satisfaction, raising efficiency or improving productive performance, raising productivity, reducing equipment or property maintenance or new alternation much of expenditure spending, office or warehouse or any workplace space planning arrangement .

However, every organization will need a facility manager or manage whose team effectively . When a facility manager begins to apply FM techniques to solve business problems. The case for FM is made. It is a simple matter of demonstrating a qualifiable return ont the investment reqired. Every organization's success, FM operation consits of three key activities: they include: needing a proper understanding of the organization's needs, wants, drivers and goals and knowing when needs to review its changing circumstances, developing an effective facilities solution o support the organization's needs, wants , property drives and contribute to achieve its goals both short term and long term, achievement of reliable delivery of that solution in a managed, measured manner.

So, it bring one question: What are the influential factors to be followed the right direction to FM manager's strategic FM operational decision? The influending factors may include: ownership, governance sector, complexity and perhaps of most signifiance, the size of the organization's property portfolio.

In fact, major occupiers feel FM service need, they are large corporate organizations and public service organizations. Their aims ususally are to raise. The most marginal improvement in efficiency or effectiveness, these aims are the great signifiance. Major property occupiers will already have a facilities department or individuals performing the FM function with another department like property, finance or human resource, sale and marketing's facilities.

Usually these FM need occupiers who will encounter this problem: How can apply FM service systems and processes to be developed to improve reliable service delivery making use of the economies of scale, not suffering because of the size of the problem. This question will be facility manager individual concerning queston: How to apply (FM) technique to solve the improvement reliable service delivery making use of the economics of scale problem for whose organization?

In reality much of extral facilities management benefits to organizations, instead of raising efficiency, improving performance, raising productivity, reducing maintenance expenditure, e.g. energy saving, reducing natural resource waste, increasing local employment, improving supply chain management are all elements of the FM contribution to every organization's need. Hence are the work life balance agrument and provision of an effective and safe working environment that supports why some organizations feel need (FM) service to support their organizational development.

Moreover, on cost benefit of space saving efficient view point, space serice cost reduction is a key driver for all organizations and the medium, or large sized players will benefit directly from a well coordinated facilities strategy. For example, application FM technique to help warehouse or office space area to save 50% space vacancy to let employees can move easily or putting enough furniture or equipment or many stocks can be putted in warehouses . So, paying more rent expenditure to rent or purchasing another new warehouse or office to satisfy workers or employees' working environment to be better need. If the organization has effective (FM) technique, then it has enough space vacancy to supply to the increase stocks number to be puttd inside in warehouse and it can let workers to move safety in available to let staffs to move easily and equipment have enough space to be stored in the limited warehouse space problem.

For greater space savings benefits will bring either long term renting or buying of increasing offices or warehouse number expenditure problem to any organizations, when the organizations' cost or renting or buying accommodation probably accounting for 60 to 70% of total occupancy cost . So a strategic programme to release space or the prevent the acquisition of moves can be the most significant consideration to any facility manager, with between 40% and 60% of the workplaces are unoccupied in most offices or warehouses at any given moment in time. Hence, how to apply (FM) technique to save space occupied areas for employment moving or stocks or equipment saving need in offices or warehouses. This issue will be any facility managers‘ seeking methods to solve problem. However, the important major advantage of facility management to organizations is that the application of management principle to keep the organization's property assets with the aim of maximizing their potentials. Thus, any organizations' facilities have become important, due to the property facilities‘ worth will increase if the organization's facility management technique can protect the organization's facilities have good performance. Then, the organization's maintenance expenditure will reduce and it won't need to spend expenditure to buy any new facilities to replace old facilities , due to they often damage factor when they are used old.

In conclusion, it explains why effective FM combines resources and activities can raise work environment improvement, which is essential to the raising employee performance aim. For hotel living service case example, this industry must need have good facility management service because hotels must need to fully equipped in term sof facilities for effectivenesses to satisfy hotel living clients' demand , hotels ought need good facilities asset management style lead to effectivenesses in service delivery, there are benefit derivable from the adoption of facilities management from which other hotels can learn from for their effective operations. Hence, it explains why effective FM can bring benefits to hotels‘ properties to be more comfortable, beautiful appearances to attract many hotel customers to choose to live the hotel. Because hotel's building industrial kitchens, rooms facilities, equipment , halls of categories, restaurent faciltiies, gum sport entertainment centers' facilities, fans, elevators, lifts, electrical installation, escalators, baking equipment, recreational facilities, including golf courses which will be important factors to influence hotel clients‘ comfortable living feeling, if the hotel can keep its all facilities in the best living environment often. Then, it can raise chance to attract many hotel customers to choose it to live. So , hotel industry has absolute need to implement effeftive FM strategy to keep its properties more attractive to satisfy its clients' living needs.

Instead of hotel industry, logistic transportation industry also needs effective facilities management in warehouse, because of the logistic company's warehouse 's facilities are good, then it will assist to raise employee individual efficiency in the safe and system sheleves stored facilities in workplace environment and improving peformance.

Consequently, it will bring the shorten time to deliver any products to clients to avodi the delaying time delivery in order to let customers to feel more satisfactory to their services. In simple, it seems that some industries need have effective facilities management techniques to help them to bring long term customer satisfactory feeling, worker individual efficiency raising and performance improvement benefits. Hence, it seems facility management techniques' demand will be increased to some industries in popular in the future because it has help to raise employee individual efficiency , productive performance and client individual satisfactory level consequently.

CHAPTER X

How to impact of workplace management on well-being and productivity

In facility management strategy, design can lead promotion, the value of offices that are enriched, particularly including warehouses, shopping centers to raise their market value. Moreover, effective organizations, such as raising powering workers when giving the effective design of office space. I assume that a good design of an interior office workspace environment seems a psychological department to influence staff individual emotion to bring positive power in order to raising productive efficient influence, such as in a commercial city office. So, it brings this question: How workspace managemet strategy can impact on staff's working behaviors in office.

In fact, office tasks general include various forms of productivity, e.g. information processing, information management and any clerical tasks by computerization. Hence, office productivity concerns how to influence each office white color worker applies computers to work in office. The office space can impact on white color workers' performances in these several aspects: feeling of psychological comfort, organizational physical comfort and job satisfaction and productivity, efficiency. So, it seems that office workspace design strategy can influence white color workers' working behavior and attitude and performance indirectly.

The office space management includes: how to removal from the workspace of everything except the materials required to do the job at hand, how tight managerial control of the workspace, and how to implement standardization of managerial practice and workspace design. So, these key ideas will influence how each white color worker's efficiency and productivity in office working environment.

For this office space design situation, a large unseparated small space size's space design can accommodate more people and so brings itself to economies of scale. As a result, space occupancy can be centrally managed with minimal disruptive interference from office workers. Indeed, many businesses now adopt a clean and fresh air office working polocy because they hace more employees than they have spaces at which they can work. This desks are either taken on a first -come first -served basis. (hot desking) or can be booked in advance. So , when a company has many employees need to work in a small space working environment. It must concern how to let staffs to feel more comfortable in order to reduce high psychological pressure to work in this uncomfortable working environment. Hence, it explains why workspace design can impact on office workers' performance in some offices. All these issues are assumed that empowering workers to manage and have input into the designn of their own workspace, then the effective office or any working places space management will enhance wellbeing to bring workers' positive emotions and improving productivity. I also assume the space working environment design hace relationship of these dependant variable factors to influence office worker individual productive efficiency. The variable factors may include psychological comfort, organizatonal comfortable, job satisfaction, physical comfort and productivity.

However, office furniture , facilities will influence office white color workers' performance ,e.g. the room size whether is big or small for manage office worker, a high backed, comfortable leather chair is needed for office staffs to sit down to let more comfortable, the door and most of the walls need glass, the office room environment needs have sea-grass rug beneath the desk covering the immediate working area, the office also needs have plants and pictures, mail boxes, telephone and computer facility is needed. When one staff needs to send email or phone call or send letters or deliver documents conveniently. These office elements are essential in order to increase physical well-being and feeling of satisfaction to whire-color workers. Hence, geen office and office working space design management is needed in order to influence white color workers' productive efficiency in long term.

Effective workspace design can influence communication to raise productivity

Office white-color workers often need communication between their managers, supervisors, and themselves. Office communication extends from the way that a user experiences a service. An effective office communication can bring these benefits; Providing positive influence on decision making by presenting a strong point of view and developing mutual understanding, delivering efficient decisions and solutions by providing accurate , timely and relevant information, enabling mutually benficial solutions, building health relationships by encouraging trust and understanding between the high level, middle level and low level staffs.

Effective office communication needs to clearly communicate its nature and purpose. Good communication ensures that all service staffs are sending out the same messages. Communication is also important for ensuring the service understands what users requires and why he/she talks about understanding users' needs and communication receiver can have effective communication skill to understand what he/she needs the another to do and the another knows he/she ought how to work by his/her task demand. Then, it will shorten much time. If the office has 100 staffs need to often communicate. However, if the office has good space managment arrangement to let every staff can communicate easily and walks to anywhere to find the right staff to communicate conveniently. Then, they can spend less time to waste on communication issue. Then, their productive efficiency will be also influence to raise.

Health and safe work environment influences productivity

Is a health and safe work environment can raise employees' work productive efficiencies indirectly? How and why it can influence employees' productive performance? Some occupations' working environments are easier to occur occupational accidents and diseases risks when the workers are working in the high health and safe risk's working environment. Hence, health and safety issues at these high life risk workplaces can be considered as a key to influence employees' overall performance. The idea that health and safety management programmes have positive impacts on productivity.

When one worker needs to work in this high risk of healh and safe workplace. He/she will consider whether how his/her work behavior will bring suffer serious infuries for shorter or longer time from work related causes in possible. So, he/she will work carefully in order to avoid injuries occurrence chance. It is possible to influence whose work performance, low productive efficiency in order to avoid any occupational accident occurrences in the dangerous workplace.

If the employee feels danger whenn he/she needs to stay in the warehouses stable location to work often. Then his/her absenteeism day number will have increase, due to he/she feels that workplace accidents and occupational illnesses and can lead to permanent occupational disability, when he/she needs to attend the stable dangerous workplace to work in the warehouse. Hence, he/she will choose to apply holiday often in order to avoid injuries chance increasing when he/she needs to stay in the stable workplace location in the warehouse. It explains why companies increase need qualified, motivated and efficient workers who are able willing to contribute activity to technical and organizational innovations. So, healthy workers working in healthy working conditions are thus an important precondition for organization to work smoothly and productively. Hence, a health and safety workplace environment can bring these benefits to organizations as below:

It can prevent among workers of learning work, due to health problems caused by their working conditions, the protection of workers in their employment from risks resulting from factors adverse to health. The placing and maintenance of the worker in an occupational, environment adapted to his/her physiological and psychological, capabilities, mental , physical and social conditions of workplace and adequay of health and safety measures are needed to any employes in order to bring positive impact not only on safety and health performance, but also productivity. However, identifying and quantifying these effects will difficult to be measured as well as the quality of a working environment has a strong influence on productive efficiency.

For one aviation air plane manufacturing factory, where workplace can environment will have high risk to occur occupational related accidents to cause employees' injuries. Hence, employees will be consider themselves safety when they need to work in high accident occurrence workplace. The bad consequence will influence such as adsenteeism day number increases, leaving this kind of aviation air plance job of employees number increases, low productive efficiencies, due to there are many proficient experienced employees who choose leave this kind of high accident risk occupation.

Consequently, any high accident occurrence risk workplace environment , employers need have good safe and health strategy to let their employees hace confidence to work in this kind of high risk accident occurrence workplace if they expect low productive efficiencies effect is caused by high accident occurrence risk workplace factor.

Is empowerment one good method to raise employee himself/herself effort in order to improve productive efficiency in organizations. Empowerment often consists of support groups, e.g. management's effective leading or trainer's training, course educational opportunities. Employee self-management education may impact to improve himself/herself job performance, e.g. increased self-empowerment, self-management skills and job treatment satisfaction.

Only organization's empowerment strategy can lead every employee to through improvements in the employee individual decision making efficacy, improvement task performance behavior by reviewing whether what are the employee himself/herself errors when he/she encounters any job difficulties, after he/she reviewed his/her task error and his/her manager feels his/her performance can be improved. Then, it can enhance satisfaction with the employee and his/her manage relationship and better access and raising efficient performance in possible . Hence, empowerment can let every employee to discover whether what task related difficulties he/she faces or encounters every day. When his/her maager give ideas to let him/her to know how he/she ought review his/her task error in a supportive education working environment, it aims to let the low performance or low inefficient employees to increase confidence to continue work in the organization. So, the employee turnover number will decrease , if the inefficient employees can feel that they can attempt to solve their task-related difficulties successfully by themselves. So, empowerment can increase social support, leadership and advocacy development , it has resulted in greater employee individual performance psychological empowerment, autonomy and authority to let every employee to feel to achieve to improve themselves efficiencies more effectively in any organizations.

For hospital organizational efficiency measurement empowerment influence case, how empowerment can influence hospital's efficiency raising? Efficiency is one of the most important indicators of hospital performance evaluation. Why do some hospitals' efficiencies poor? It is possible that mismangement of resources, lacking health plan packages, e.g. coverage of basic health insurance, poor quality of care service, more payment demand for out-of pocket payment , quality of primary healthcare , healthcare providers neglect to concern potentially about service efficiency issues.

In fact, low hospital efficiency is the major problem to influence patients number to choose the hospital's medical service, e.g. when the hospital often needs patients to queue to wait for doctor's care medical service. They need to wait on hour at least or more when the hospital has many patients are waiting for its medical service. Then,it will influence them to choose another hospital to replace it , if the hospital 's medical fee is cheaper and it does not need patients to spend long time to queue to wait its medical service. So, service efficiency is important to influence patients consumers' positive or negative feeling to choose the hospital's medical service. Even, the hospital's doctors are famous ot they own many medical working experience, if patients often need long time to queue to wait its medical service . Then, it will cause its patients number to be reduced .

These arre variable factors to influence the hospital's inefficiency. They may include old speed hospital information system and medical record documents based on inefficienct input and output variables. Input variables may include the number of hospital admissions, the number of nurses and the number of available beds. The output variable may include average of length of stay and bed turnover interval inefficient paper document record in the patient record admistrative department.

However, to evaluate the hospital efficiency indicators may include technical, scale and managerical efficiency the out-based data development analysis apprach and the variable returns to scales assumption was used. Based on the out-input based approach (maximizing the factors of medical service production), to increse efficiency the organization should be increased outputs.

Hence, when the hospital has good efficient evaluation method to measure every staff's performance , e.g. ward administrative clerk, patient registration clerk etc. Then, it can base on an put-put based approach and assuming a variable return to scale, there is capacity to improve technical efficiency and managerial efficiency in these any hospital different administrative units without an increase in costs and use of same amount of resources in relation to technical efficiency and managerial efficiency and scale efficiency of hospital's administrative labour individual task.

In conclusion, factors, such as modification of managerical practices, use of modern technologies tailored to the cultural, politicsal and formulation of clinical guidelines to standardize the medical processes in order to reduce medical errors and increase the empowerment of health care buyers (insurance organizations), length of stay, management hospitals by specialist managers, administrative requirement, full time hospital physicians, limiting the authority of decision makers in relation to the recruitment of staff in accordance with the needs of the hospital and optimal allocation of beds, conducting economic evaluations and the type of hospitals ownership had an impact on the hospital efficiency significantly. By increasing the number of beds the hospitals efficiency decreases. Otherwise, optimizing the bed size can increase hospital efficiency.

However, the important factor to raise hospital overall staffs efficiencies empowerment is needed to let every hospital staff to review whether why and how himself/herself error is caused and he/she needs to review his/her errors to avoid to be caused from any negligence again in order to avoid patients' complaints again or reduce the patients' complaint number aims. So, empowerment of staff himself/herself error review factor is one major raising efficient good method.

In psychological view ,in any organization's environments, they depend on the types of social and physical environment factors to influence employee personal behavior how to be caused. How and why does the employee select to do whose behavior? If the organization's physical and social environment is better, then it may influence its employees select to work hard. It is possibe to bring productive efficient raising consequence.

In fact, when one new employee enters the new organization to work, he/she needs to learn how to adapt to cooperate with the organization's old employees to work together. So, it explains how and why organizaion's physical and social environment can influence the new employee individual motivation of behavior to work. In regarding new employee individual behavior by new employer's culture expectations as well as new employees need to adapt of actions that are likely to productive positive outcomes and generally discard those that bring unrewarding or pubishing outcomes by new employer's treatment.

However, anticipated material and organization environment co-operation outcomes between the new employee and the organization old employees' cooperation, which are not the only kind of incentives that influence the new employee behavior of the new employee actions were performed only on behalf of anticipated external rewards and pubishment from the new employer. In actuality, the new employee concerns considerable self-direction in the face of the new employer's organization's old employees competing influences. However, when the new employee has adopted an intension and an action plan. When, he/she works in the new organization for a period, he/she can't simply not back and visit for the appropriate performances to appear.

The new employee's new job goal will be motivated by enlisting self-evaluative engagement in activities rather than directly. By making self-evaluation conditional on matching personal new job standards, the new employee will give direction to his/her new job pursuits and create self-inventives to sustain his/her efforts for new job goal attainmet. The new employee will select to do new task behavior to give him/her self-satisfaction and a sense of pride and self worth for the new job chance.

Efficacy beliefs also play a key role in shaping the new employees' behavior to do their tasks by influencing the types of new organization's activities and working environments, the new employees choose to set into any factor that influences the employee's choice behavior can affect the direction of employee personal career development in the new organization. This is because the organizational working environment influences operating in the employee how to select working environments continue to work. Thus, by choosing and shaping the new organization's working environments, new employee can have a hand in what they expect.

In conclusion , when a new employee chooses the new organization to work. He/she must need to adapt the organization's new working environment. If he/she feels difficult to adapt or accept to the organization's new working environment, then he'she will be influenced to work inefficient or poor productive performance , due to he/she feels unhappy to work the new organization's working environment and the new organization's manager will dissatisfy his/her performance and complain or give verbal warning to dismiss him/her. Then, it will bring the poor consequence to let the organization's inefficient productive performance effect. If many new employees feel difficult to adapt to work in the new organization. Then, inefficient productive performance will be influenced to keep a long term. So, it implies that the organization will need to change its organizationa culture in order to let many new employees can adapt and accept this new organizationla culture to work happily if the organization expects new employees work to raise productive efficiency successfully.

Chapter Four

HR Development Improves Performance

What is efficient achievement of technological inputs factor in construction industry

What is organizational efficient raising actual mean? I shall indicate construction industry case to explain technological factor is the major factor to assist construction organization to raise efficiency. For construction industry example, improved productivity could be attributed to advances in and increased usage of information technologies, increased competition, due to globalization and changes in workplace and organizational structures.

For construction efficiency, the construction process can reduce waste in coordinating labor and in managing, moving and installing materials, loss avoidance. It can achieve efficient aim. The construction productive efficient concept can be defined efficiency improvements as ways to cut waste and labor. So, one construction organizational efficient achievement means that it implemented through the capital facilities sector, these activities would significantly advance construction efficiency and improve the quality, timeliness, cost effectiveness of projects in construction processes.

On construction industry technological factor influence hand, it can influence that construction productivity how well, how quality, and at what cost buildings and infrastructure can be constructured, directly affects prices for homes and consumer products and the robustness of the national economy. Construction productivity will also affect the outcomes of national efforts to renew existing infrastructure systems; to build new infrastructure for power from renewable to renew existing infrastructure systems; to build new infrastructure for power from renewable resources to develop high-performance " green building" and to remain competitive in the global market. If the construction organization expected to achieve effficient aim. It ought consider how to change in building design, construction and renovation and in building materials and materials recycling, will be essential to the success of national efforts to minimize environmental impacts, reduce overall energy use, and reduce greenhouse gas emissions.

However, construction industry analysts differ on whether construction industry productivity is improved by efficiency outcome. They indicate construction efficiency needs to reduce 25-50 percent waste in coordinating labour and in managing, moving and installing materials. This is the most minimum standard efficient achievement level to any construction organizations.

What are the factors influence efficiency to any construction organizations? An efficient construction task process is made possible by a range of information technological tools and applications, including computer-aided design and drafting, three and four dimensional visualization and modeling programs, laser scanning, cost-estimating and scheduling tools and materials tracking. So, high technological tool will assist to raise efficient construction process to any construction organizations. It can help them to shorten time and avoid materials waste and control cost effective estimation for any construction projects.

Effective use of interoperate technologies requires effective team cooperative processes and effective planning up front and this it can help overcome obstacles to efficiency created by process fragmentation. Interoperable technologies can also help to improve the quality and speed of any construction project related decision making, integrate processes, managing supply chains, sequence work flows, improve data accuracy and reduce the time spent on data entry, reduce design and engineering conflicts and the subsequent need for rework, improve the life-cycle management of buildings and infrastructure.

All of these factors will influence whether the construction organization can implement efficiency in success. For example, interoperable techcholgies include legal issues, data-storage capacities and the need for " intelligent " search applications to sort quickly through thousands of data elements and make real-time information available for on-site decision making. How to improve job-site efficiency through more effective interfacing of people, processes, materials ,equipment, and information. The job site for a large construction project is a dynamic place, involving numerous contractors, subcontractors, trades people and labors, all of whom must require equipment, materials and supplies to complete their tasks. So, they need to know how to manage activities and demands to achieve the maximum efficiency from the limited available resources. Time, money, and resources will have possible to be wasted when projects are poorly managed, causing workers to have to wait around for tools and work crews are not on-site at appropriate time or when supplies and equipment are stored in complexity or difficulty, requiring that they can be moved multiple time (time waste).

How to improve job site safety and improve the quality of projects, significantly cut waste? The use of automated equipment, e.g. for excavation and earthmoving operations, pip installation, concrete placement, and information technologies, e.g. radio-frequency identification tags for tracking materials personal digital assistants for capturing field data. These high technological tool can help any construction projects to raise efficiency to process improvements and the provision for real -time information for improved management at the job site.

Moreover, on mannal research and development tools hand, instead of data technological tools hand, any construction organizations also need to consider how to take a variety of forms: How to test field on a job site? How to arrange lecture shows in efficient way, seminrs, training and conference, and scientific laboratories time, human resource available arrangement, spending expenditure budget to finish. Moreover, effective performance mearements are enablers of innovation and of corrective actions throughout a construction project's life cycle. They can help any construction companies or organizations understand how processes led to success or failure, improvements or inefficiencies and how to use that knowledge to improve construction products , processes and outcomes of active projects.

The nature of construction projects, the industry itself, any construction organizations ought consider the construction working environment how to influence construction workers' emotions. For example, when the construction site is high levels, of noise, dust and airborne particles, adverse weather conditions,and other factors that can cause injuries and thereby reduce efficiency and productivity. New types of equipment can make an active physically easier to perform, easier to control, move precise , and safer for construction workers. Similarly, changes in materials can reduce the weight of construction components, make them easier to handle, move and install. Manufacturing building components off-site providers need more control conditions and allow for improved quality and precision in the fabrication of the component, One study that examined the relationship between changes in material technology and construction productivity based on 100 construction a related tasks, the study found that labor productivity for the same activity increased by 30 % at least when higher materials were used and labour productivity also improved when construction activites were performed using materials that were easier to install or were pre-fabricated. So, it seems material heavy can influence construction worker individual productive efficiency in site, if the material is higher , then the construction worker's productivity will be influenced to improve (Goodrum et al. 2009).

Thus, the factors influence construction organization's efficiency. It focuses on whether the construction firm applies how advanced construction technologies to assist its construction workers to work as well as whether its construction environment can let workers to feel safe to avoid life danger or accident occurrence. When the workers do not worry about whose life safety as well as they can apply advanced construction technology to assist them to work. Then, their productive efficiencies ought need to be improved easily. Thus, facility management and advanced technology will be the main factor to raise construction workers' efficiencies.

Can effective departmental communication
factor influence successful organizational
effective change

In any organizations, their staffs must need communication either between the supervisor and low level staff(s) or between the same level staff(s) himself/herself/themselves. Has it relationship between communication and organizational efficient change? Can effective communication bring advantages to improve effort of employees to raise productive efficiency and execute change strategies more effective? Does organizational efficient change depend on effective communication in overall organization from low to top level, or top to low level? Why does effective overall organizational communication raise efficiency?

It is possible to consider that poorly managed change communication results in rumors and resistance to let every employee to know whether he/she ought know how to do it in order to finish whose task efficiently and effective result aim. Otherwise, an effective communication can let the employee to understand whether he/she needs how to do it clearly. Then, he/she will be possible to finish his/her task efficiently. So, it seems that employee individual job satisfaction will bring positive (effective) organizational outputs or negative (ineffective) organizational outputs, when he/she can be often communicated either efficiently or inefficiently.

In one big organization, if every employee feels difficult to communicate daily. Then, it is possible to influence his/her low productive , or inefficient performance. So, managers, supervisors and low level staffs ought have effective communication between them. Communication can include writing communication,e.g. memos are needed to delivered between internal different departments or between external departments daily immedicately by the delivered staff. Because it will influence the department delivers what message to another department to know to be delayed if the memo can not delivered to the department on the day. Then, it may influence inefficiency. Communication can include oral or verbal. The supervisor or manager ought take hir/her low level staff how to do the task to be improved immediately if he/she feels that the staff her error. If he/she can't tell the staff to let him/her to know whether he/she ought need how to do to be better. Then, it will cause the employee does not know whether what his/her error is and he/she ought need how to review to change his/her error to be right or reasonable acceptance in order to satisfy her/his supervisor/manager's task need. So, it seems that effective communication can influence how the staff's performance indirectly. Due to his/her misunderstanding how to do whose task to be improved or better. Then, it will bring inefficiency outcome in possible.

Any organizations need to depend on achievement of efficiency and effectiveness of themselves staffs communication behaviors every day. During the staffs' communication , they will face problems of different understanding of communication related issues. Communication is either thus, such as negative communication phenomena that must be prevented or avoided; examples of difficult communication channel unavoidable problematic phenomena within the organization; they result from person/personality communication problems of participants or as positive (creative) phenomena that enable the organization's development. For example: the both different departments or single department communicator(s) can present in possibility to active more effective communication participation and they can encourage creation of new and opportunities, as well as they can contribute significantly to introduction of changes; when they enable additional forms of either verbal/oral or writing form of memo or report communication. For example, when one marketing team needs to write a report to recommend new idea concerns hoe to promote the new product to the global market. If the marketing team member can cooperate to discuss easily. Then, they can communicate how to gather data to cooperate how to communicate to sale team members in order to achieve sale target easily. Hence, when the marketing team members can communicate to sale team members to give ideas to let them to know what their new marketing plan will be implemented in order to follow their marketing plan to prepare how to sell their firm's new products strategically. When the organization is large size, e.f. IBM computer organization , the marketing team members will need effective communication to sale team members if they expect to implement any new product market plan to promote to sell to global computer users more easily/ If the IBM large computer organization sale department members need to spend much time to contact marketing department members in person. Then, due to difficult communication problem causes their plan to implement the marketing promotion plan in long time. It seems that marketing and sale departments' staffs inefficient performance, it is due to ineffective communication between departments in possible.

Moreover, ineffective or different communication environment also causes individual conflicts impact organization in different ways(e.g. indirectly , directly) are of different importance to influence the organization's overall different department cooperation relationship to be poor (e.g. highly urgent communication matter, less important communication matter). They organization's different departments may not know whether what is the highly urgent matter needs to be dealt immediately and what is the less important matter does not need to be delat immediately of the organization's department staffs feel difficult to communicate, due to time management is poor causes the department staffs do not know whether the department staffs ought spend time to do the communication tasks with another department staffs in prior in order to let the another department staffs know how they ought to follow their demand to finish their task in short time cooperation efficiently. Thus, effective communication can help the organization to effectiveness present the level at which the organization achieves its goals , when its different department staffs can communicate to cooperate to work team work to finish effectively any tasks effectively and efficiently in short time. So, effective departmental communication can bring the limited staffs number the benefit, such as invested less efforts and less time input to help the organization to achieve the most maximum outcome output of its aims and goals of the organization. The effective communication concerns the staff's communication behavioral factor, e.g. (message content) inputs, (writing or verbal communication method) operations, and (how long time to finish the mission) outputs relation between the factors (internal, external departments).

In conclusion, when one organization has many different departments as well as many staffs who need to often cooperate to communicate how to do evey task together. Time management is one important successful factor to every department individual staff, he/she needs to know whether what is the highly urgent important messages are needed to be communicated to let the another department staffs to know, that is the less important messages are needed to be communicated to the another department staffs to know. Hence, effective communication is concerned how the employee arranges time to work daily. If the employee is one poor time management person, then his/her communication will ineffective, the consequence will bring the organization's different departments' cooperation inefficiency ,even it can cause the organization's overall productive performance to be poor, due to long term inefficient departmental difficult communication between departments factor.

Can human resource development training factor influence organizational productive performance

Can HRD has relationship efficiency of HRD training and development in organization growth? HRM is the function within an organization that focused on recruitment of management of and provision of direction to people who work in the organization, performance measurement and rewarding management of effective HRM enables employees to contribute effectively and productivity to the overall company direction and the achievement of the organization's goals and objectives in possible.

How any why effective HRD can influence organizational efficiency? HRD is administrative activities with HR planning , recruitment , selection, training , appraisal , motivation, reward strategic focuses on employees. So employees are any organization's assets. It assumes that when the organization's employees (assets) can be trained effectively. Then, the assets (employees) efficiencies will raise in long term. HRM designs the effective activities to be arranged to provide to every employee individual task and coordinates , all human element within the organizations. When, every employee individual effort can be attributed to the most maximum . Then, it assumes the organizational overall efficiency will be raised. So, effective training is one suggestive method aims to raise employee individual effort level to the maximum. Then, the organization's overall efficiency will be raised in possible. However, HRD of training needs to be spent much money to invest in large size organizatons. Although, large size organizations, e.g. IBM computer firs, its training provides to spend much expenditure to train computer programming staffs to teach them how to create different new softwares in order to raise its competitive effort, it is long time investment value to its computer programming staffs because it is possible that it can upgrade its computer programming staffs' creative programming skills to be invented any new kinds of software products or designing new kinds of computers to sell. Hence, IBM 's HRD in training function has difficult evaluation its future human element of programming staffs' worth in long term. When, its programming staffs' skills can be upgraded to create special software products. Then, its overall staffs' efficient performance will also be raised because their software creative skills have been improved, due to effective training provision.

Effective training can solve the challenges of lack of skilled labour, heavy competition among firms, technological problems, low productivity and poor product implementation when placing a serious limitation on product expansion and increase in productivity. So, effective training needs have these characteristics: The trainer needs have good teaching skills or methods to raise employss individual creative effort, the training's content must need useful to satisfy the trainees' task need. So, the HRD's factors, such as organizational culture, job satisfactin, training and development and stress will have close relationship to influence the organization's overall employee productive performance or efficiency to be raised. For IBM computer example, it's organizational culture is that encouraging different department computer professionals create themselve software designing effort, providing effective training courses to raise their software designing creative effort in order to raise efficiency to achieve how to create new softwares in short time efficiently. Then, their job satisfaction may be increased, due to they feel that their software creative efforts and writing programming skillsa re raised or improved. Their stress will be also reduced, due to they do not need to worry about when they can create any new kinds of softwares or computer engineering systems to be invented to sell. So, if the IBM's HRD 's training function is one effective training course, it can assist IBM's programmers to raise their software and hardware creative effort to achieve raising IBM organization's overall productive performance and every software and hardware employee individual efficiency is also raised in possible.

Hence, any organization's training (HRD) will be one successful factor to influence the firm's productive performance and efficiency in possible. An organization's HRD of training and development function concerns with organizational activity aimed at improvement of organizational performance, including employee development, human resource learning and development. Training has traditionally been defined as the process by individuals change their skills, knowledge, attitudes, and/or behavior. Similarly, training involves designing and supporting learning activities that result in a desired level of performance. In constrast, HRD refers to long-term growth and learning, directing attention more on what an individual may need to know or do at some future time. In fact, training focuse more on current job duties or responsibilities, development points to future jon responsibilities. It emphasizes either the product of training and development or how individuals perform as a result of what they have learned.

However, an effective training is real an educational process, trainees can learn new information, re-learn and re-improve existing knowlege and skills , and more importantly have time to think and consider what new options can help them improve their effectiveness and performance at work in possible. Effective trainings are taught useful information that inform employees and develop skills and behaviors that can be transferred back to the workplace. The goals of training is to create an impact to cause the consequence , such as inefficiency can be changed to efficiently as well as ineffectiveness can be changed to effectiveness of the training itself's final goal. An effective training, the focus is on creating specific action steps and commitments that focus trainee's attention on incorporating their new skills and ideas back at work. However, training can be offered as skill development for individuals and groups. In general, trainings involve presentation and learning of content as a means for enhancing skill development and improving workplace behaviors.

These are both processes, training and development are often closely connected. Training can be used as a method for developing or improving or creating or upgrading skills and expertise to prevent problems from arising and can be an effective tool to reduce the performance gaps among staff . Training learning development can be used to create solutions to workplace issues, before or after the trainee had encountered any problems when they are working. Hence, an effective human resource training development can help the organization's overall employees on a team, in a department and as part of an institution identify effective strategies for improving performance. Also, it means that when the organization's employees overall performances are improved or efficiencies are raised, it may be concerned to an effective training is provided to teach them before in possible. It implies that how to measure whether the training is effective, it is decided by whether the organization's overall efficiency is raised or not. If the organization's employees overall productive performance whom are improved. Its efficiency is raised, then it is possible that it had implemented an effective training to provide them to learn useful knowledge to raise their creative effort to solve their job-related problems in possible.

Thus, it seems that it has relationship between training and efficiency to any organizations. HRD process aims to find ideas and solutions that can effectively return the group to a state of high performance. Training and HRD describes the formal, ongoing efforts that are made within organizations to improve the performance and the employer self-fulfillment of himself/herself through a variety of educational methods and programmes. Hence, in the modern workplace, training development process indicates that the trainer needs to teach from short term specific job skills to long term professional development.

All of above issues, they are based on these assumptions , such as these relationships: There is a relationship between organizational culture and employee performance, there is a relationship between job satisfaction and employee performance, there is a relationship between stress and employee performance as well as there is a relationship between training and development and employee performance. However, training and development is the main factor to improve employee performance. When the organization has effective training and development to provide to its employees (trainees) to learn , then their stress will be influenced to reduce, job satisfaction can b raised and they can accept to adapt their organizational culture more easily. Then, their efficiencies will raise more when they can perform better or improve performance between to compare their prior work performance in their organizations. Hence, training and development element will be the most influential element to compare the other organizational culture, job satisfaction and stress elements in a human resource management factor, which can influence whole firm performance (every employee individual performance) obviously. Because I assume when the organization can have an effective training and development deparrment to provide any kinds of effective training courses to let its employees (trainees) to learn. Then, it is possible that it can help all employees (trainees) to increase themselves confidence to work more easily. Due to an effective training development can influence they can accept more easier adaption to their organizational culture, bring more job satisfaction, when they feel more easier to do their tasks and their stress will also be reduced, when their any job-related difficulties will be solved every day. The final consequence will being that the organization's every employee (trainee) whom efficiency will be raised in possible as well as it will bring the firm's overall employees performances to be raised or improved or the firm itself overall performance to be raised or improved.

In conclusion, it seems that an effective training and development can assist the organization's employee(trainee) individual efficiency to be raised or improved, then it can assist the firm itself overall employees(trainees) whose performace to be raised or improved, due to the effective training can influence the trainees overall efficiency to be raised or improved, then it can influence the firm itself overall performance to be raised or improved in possible.

Factors influence employee motivation
to achieve organizational effective
performance

In fact, one organization can influence employee motivation, instead of external fairly management workplace environment, effective training provision better reward attractive strategies, fair performance measurement policy, accurate selection and recruitment interview method factors. The intrinsic factors that are also importance to influence employee motivation. For example, employee achievement and recognition work itself satisfaction, role and responsibility itself, salary structure, the level to which the employee feels appreciated and the building good or bad relationship between the employee and his/her supervisor or manager. There are influential psychological factor to impact on the employee performance in the organization.

Motivatin is the personal intrinsic emotion factor how to influence the employee to develop a certain mind set regarding his/her job. In fact, the exterinsic factors in the organization's human resource management practices particularly to ensure that the employees are influenced well motivated to perform their tasks. In addition, the organization may need extrinsic factors, such as encouraging employee involvement in the decision making participation and innovation in the decision making participation and innovation and increases the promotion appreciation or effective or useful training opportunities for the personal growth: It can positively influence the intrinsic factors of employee motivation.

Similarly, when one employee feels he/she acknowledges his/her role in important to influence on organizationa; effectiveness in order to assist the organization to overcome challenges, it can create a strong and positive job cooperation relationship with its employees as well as improving task fulfillment and ensure they have job satisfaction. In special, any large size organizations, they have low, middle and top level staffs. If they only feel the middle and high level management staffs too feel their roles are important , but they neglect to let the low level staffs, e.g. workers, clerks , salespeople, teacher etc. low level staffs. These staffs themseleves can also feel their roles are important in their organizations. Then, these large size organizations' effectiveness or efficiency or performance will be poor, due to these large size organizations feel they are not important staffs and they can be replaced from other new employees any time easily. Then, these low level staffs will have plan to find another organization (new employee) to replace their current employers any time. In the consequence, the organizations will be possible to lose any one of these important low level high efficient or good performance staffs (workers) or main HR asset. It will lead to failure of these organizations when these high efficient staffs (workers) high staff turnover number is increasing. The reason is because they feel that they hace hgh efficiency, so they can another new job very easily. So they have poor job satisfaction, due to their orgaizations can not motivate their low level staffs take more reward and good salary to attract them to work efficiently. These emplers do not understand the benefits of motivation in the workplace, then the investment in these low level employee related policies ca be easily justified. They only consider to satisfy the middles and top level managemet staffs' tasks need and reward need. If these low level employees are motivated to fulfill their tasks and achieve their goals, e.g. the organization's salespeople don't attmept to help their organization to sell their products hardly, the school's teachers do not attempt to find good teaching behavioral method to attract their students to raise interest to learn or let they feel fun to learn from their teaching in classrooms. Then, their poor sale or teaching performance will bring the students or product buyer number to be reduced. For this reason, it is essential for a manager/supervisor to understand what really motivates the low level employees without making on improvemen performance or inefficiency or low productive assumption.

Motivation means an individual's intensity, mind set, direction and spending effort toward attaining a goal. It can be either individual goal motivation to achieve any matter or visiion from personal benefit or the organization goal motivation to persuade its employees to help it to achieve its improvement performance, raising profit, raising sale , raising productive growth, raising efficiency , vison or aim . In this chapter, I shall discuss how the organization's motivation to employees can impact organization's overall performance or efficiency or productivity to be either good or bad. So, motivation to employees can include extrinsic motivation, e.g. increasing salary level, increasing welfares, as well as intrinsic motivation , e.g. job satisfaction, appreciation, promotion chance/opportunity, feeling important role. I shall assume that if the employee lacks motivation emotion to work, then he/she will only spend less effort, nervous , time to attribute to work more hardly in the organization. Because they do not feel enjoyable to work , they won't raise efficient work performance, as well as their intrinsic motivation can not energize personal enjoyment, interest, or pleasure to let them they feel, they play one important role to earn unfair external reward to compare other same level or not same level staffs, e.g. the top level manager feels he/she earns unfair reward to compare another top level manager or the low level worker feels that he/she earn unfair reward to compare another low level worker, or the low level staff feels his/her organization gives excellent reward to the middle level or top level manager/supervisor only. So, it implies that the poor motivateion will occur to the overall organizational low middle and/or top level staffs , it is not only occur to the low level staffs. For example, if the organization's CEO feels his/her reward treatment is poor or unfair to compare to other companies' CEP reward. It means that it is possible that the organization's poor motivation or effort can be caused by the top, middle or low level staff, he /she needs to compare to othe companies; same level staff reward in general job market reward structure. Hence, any one organization needs to consider whether its reward is poor to compare other organizations' rewards. They can not only consider whether its reward is fair treatment to the low to to[level staffs issue only, but it neglects to consider whether wha tis the current market reward structure to its same competitors' rewards. It seems that one organization's employees will be possible compare whether their rewards are fair between themselves in their organizations as well as they will be possible compare whether their rewards are fair to the similar sale or service organizations or competitors. Hence, fair and reasoable reward can motivate or encourage every staff to accept to spend more effort, time, nervous to attribute to serve his/her organization.

Consequently, when the staff has good motivation, it may bring better efficiency, improving performance, raising productivity in possible. Otherwise, when the staff has bad emotivation, it may bring poor efficiency, or inefficiency, worse performance, reducing productivity in possible. So , it seems that it has indirect relationship between motivation and the organization's overall performance.

Performance measurement influences
effectiveness

Performance means understanding as achievement of the organization in relation with its set goals. It may include outcomes achieved, or accomplished through contribution of individuals or teams to the organization's strategic goals. It brings this question whether effective performance measurement can raise the organization's effectiveness. Performance has a linkage with the individual potential and how best it is realized by the individual organization needs performance measurement because it needs to measure every employee individual job behavior in order to evaluate whether his/her performance is acceptable to either raise salary/ wage or keep the same level salary/wage or appreciate to promote higher or senior position or unemploy (fire) the employee, when his/her performance is poor or unacceptable task level to earn this position level's reward with regard to manage. The employee's potential becomes the input to the productive process and performance is the out. It seems that when the one organization has many good performance employees number, then its effectiveness can not be improved to be better to compare the another similar industry organization has less good performance employees number , then its effectiveness can not improve to be better. The actua reason many include any company is one cooperative organization, it needs different teams or departments' members , workers, staffs to participate to work in low, middle, top level organizational structure. Hence, one organizational behavior can not be influenced only by one employee individual behavior or performance. The organization's overall performance or effectiveness ought be influenced by group (team) and organizational purpose, group (team) or organization capacities and resources, human climate in the group or team or the organization, the (team) group every member personal performance quality, efficient level , productive level. So, organization needs to consider how to make reasonable or fair feedback on group (team) overall performance. It does not only consider how to make reasonable or fair feedback on the top or middle level management employee individual performance only and it neglects to consider the low level employee individual performance measurement.

There are three abilities in an individual are said to be essential for performance achievement to evaluate whether the employee individual performance to excellent , good, common, poor level. They include the employee individual desire or motivation himself/herself ability, knowledge or know-how quality or action to actualize ability. Hence, one excellent performance employee whom ought have these above personal quality or ability characteristics, then he/she can perform the esscellent job performance. If the team or group or department owns the employees whom own above these abilities , then group, team, department's effectiveness will be improved, or efficiency can be raised, or productive growth can be raised more easily. However, effective performance measurement model was based mainly on financial measures and considered as one component of the planning and control cycle view, it is based on multipl non financial measures where performance measurement acts as an independent process includes in a set of activities.

How to design an effective performance measurement ? I shall assume that it has relationship between organizational effectiveness and performance measurement, also it means that whether organization is either effective or ineffective, it depends on whether its performance measurement is effective or ineffective. In essence, an organizational effectiveness represents the outcome of organizational activities when performance measurement consists of an assessment tool to measure effectiveness. In fact, the team " performance" and " effectiveness" are used interchangably because any organizational problems are related to their definition, measurement and explanation when their different groups, teams or departments' staffs are encountering the similar or same general problems when they are feeling in their departments. It seems that any organizations need to find whether what kinds of task problems to influence its different teams feel difficult to work , different department's staffs whom are feeling in general. Then, when the organization cna ensure whether what kinds of taxk problems that its staffs are facing. It can let its staffs to know how any why it needs its any ony one of its staffs to suggest useful ideas or opinions to help it to solve its organizational tasks problems in themselves department. If any one staff can know that whether he/she ought need how to do to solve whom task difficulty and the organization can attempt to use whose opinion to confirm his/her opinion is effective or useful to help it to solve his/her department general problems to its this department 's staffs' facing. Then, the organization can make more accurate judgement or evaluation to ensure the staff can be one excellent performance employee because he/she can attempt to find the effective or useful method(s) to help him/her deparment or team or group to solve his/her department overall member whom are facing or encountering general task difficulties or problems that they feel needs to solve immediately. It seems that one excellent performance employee needs own have one unique difficult solvable ability that the other members can not find the effective or useful solution method(s) to help the department to solve. Its overall daily task difficulties that its department members can not solve easily. Similarly, it means that effective or fair performance measurement is based on whether the employee can find the best solution(s0 to help whom department to solve any task problems(difficulties) when it's overall members feel whom are encountering the same problems daily. When the department has one staff whom can suggest the best opinion(s) to help the department's staffs to raise efficiency or improve productivity to achieve whose department overall performance effectiveness to be improved better. Then the department staff ought be the excellent performance staff and his/her reward must be the best to compare other same level staffs in the department. Hence, the fair or reasonable performance measurement is based on the employee individual ability, it is not based on the department overall ability. It means that one department, however, its department structure level is the low, middle or top level, even the low level department ought have one or some staff(s) whom own personal ability is above to compare the same job responsibility level staffs in the department. The owninf above-average ability staff(s) ought earn more appreciation or promotion opportunity increasing to compare the owning low-average ability staffs in the department. When the department's low-average or general ability staffs who had been working in the department long time acknowledge why the staff(s) can be appreciated to promote to do the senior position or increase salary immediately to compare themselves. Then they will be influenced by the owning above-average ability of employee(s) to work hardly or attempt to find any solution(s) or method(s) to help themselves to solve any unpredictive task difficulties in order to achieve appreciation or increasing salary or senior position promotion personal aim or desire. Then, they can influence the department's overall effectiveness to be improved in long term possible. Hence, it seems to explain one effective or good performance measurement can influence the organization's effectiveness to be improved successfully.

An effective performance measurement model needs have an effective is measured in the terms of accomplishment of the outcomes to every department, it do not neglect the importance to review its error to help its different departments to solve themselves difficulties when their any one employee individual opinion is failure or unsuccessful to help it solve whom department's prior problems, also every employee ought have chance to let himself/herself to express opinions to let it to know whether what task difficulties when he/she is possible to encounter, and it ought let every department staff has opportunity to carry on group meeting discussion how to solve himself/herself department's overall facing general problems as well as it also needs to adopt the different solutions to attempt to find which one solution is the best in order to evaluate whether whom ability is above to any one in the department. It aims to make the more accurrate performance measurement decision to give the fair and reasonable reward or welfare to any one in any department.

In conclusion, an effective performance measurement has these requirements: It needs to find whom the employee(s) has/have good decision making ability to help himself/herself department ot the other employees to solve general task difficulties in order to improve of decision process though (setting performance and strategies goals and ensuring an adequate level and mix of resources) and coordination to parts of a business to achieve objective; it needs have effective control to feedback to ensure the input-process-out system. Input means that different reward structure to be designed to the low , middle and top level employees' performance measurementevaluation and reward evaluation need, process means that an effective employee performance measurement evaluation startegic system and ouput means that an fair and reasonable reward structure implementation to every low, middle and top level employee. It is properly and to motivate and evaluate employees, managers need and it also needs to consider the overall organization how is related to its values, preferences and where themsleves department employees should be focusing their attention and energy how to attempt to solve solve themselves task difficulties in order to find whom is/are the above -average ability employee(s) in themselves department and to be recommend to appreciate to earn the more fair and reasonable reward immediately. So, an effective performance measurement organization is not only composed of individuals, but also interdependent groups with different immediate goals, (desired from specializations), different ways of working , different formal training and even different personality types. For example, staffs who work in accounting department , often have every different personality, goals , training and styles of work and socialization than staffs who work in advertising or marketing departments. So , the organization ought need to follow whether the staffs are working in which departments in order to arrange the most reasonable job task responsibilities to let him/her to work. It means that one accounting deparment will need to employ different accounting skillful staffs to do these different accounting task functions, such as financial and finance function, salary and performance measurement calcuation function, cost accounting and management budget function. So, if one employee whom is proficient on financial accounting, but he/she is arranged to do the management and cost budget function task duties. Then, it will influence whom performance to be poor, due to he/she is not proficient do do management and cost budget analysis task duties. Although, he/she has accounting knowledge and working experiences, but it does not mean that he/she has ability to do management and cost budget task duties better in the accounting department. So, any manager needs to select the right employee to arrange the right task function to let the employee do the right task responsibility duties in his /her department. If the manager selected the wrong employee to be arranged him/her to do the wrong job task reponsibility position in whose department. It is possible to influence its department's overall efficiency or productive performance to be poor.

Hence, it has close indirect relationship between performance measurement and the organization's overall effectiveness. Because effectiveness oriented companies are concerned with output, sales, quality, creation of value added, innovation, cost reduction. It measures the degree to which a business achieve its goals or the way outputs interest with the economics and social environment. When the organization has an effective or fair and reasonable performance measurement strategy. Then, its employees will feel more satisfactory to improve productive performance or efficiency in order to earn more reasonable awards easily. When the organization has many employees can improve their productive efficiency. Then, its overall productive number will be increased or service performance will be improved . Consequently, its effective performance can be also improved, thus it explains why and how when one organization has one effective performance measurement strategy , it can improve its organizational overall performance to be more effective because every department will have more employees whom like to attribute more nervous, effort, time to do themselves job duties in order to achieve appreciation, promotion, increasing salary opportunity when they acknowledge their organization has fair and reasonable performance mangement policy to evaluate themselves performance fairly.

Similarly, in one fair and reasonable performance measurement organizaional workplace environment, it will influence every department employee individual emotion to be positive, he/she can feel whom need to spend more effort, tiem and nervous to work in order to assist his/her department to raise efficiency or productivity or improve service performance aim. Then, if the organization has many department's efficiency and productive growth can be raised. It means that the organization's overall performance can be more effective also. So, it has indirect relationship between performance measurement and organizational overall performance.

CHAPTER XI

Learning human behaviors bring what economic influences

Human Behavioral network job brings social economic benefits

What does human network job mean ? Why may human network job be popular? Why human network job behavior may influence economy ?

Nowadays internet is popular to use. We can apply internet to find data , search any new things, even earn money. Why does internet

may become huma network job source. For example, e-publish may be one kind of new human network job. Any authors may apply internet

channel to help them to sell electronic or paper books from e-publisher web store. They may apply facebook, you tub etc. any online

channel to promote themselves new books to let new readers to know whether when they may buy themselves favourable new topic books to read

from electronic publisher web store.

Thus, future electronic publisher industry may help any authors to build internet network platform to help them to sell and promote

ot advertise their any one new electronic or paper book topic to let global any one reader to choose to buy their any new topic books from electronic publisher web store easily and conveniently. However, it implies that electronic network platform author may be one kind of future new human network job in our societies.

How electronic network platform author job may bring economy benefit in macro economy view? A person can have few friends, contacts and still be very influential if these few

friends and contacts are themselves highly influential, e.g. one author must not need to know any one reader in global society. When they like to choose any electronic books from electronic internet network platform. They may become the author's any one topic book buyer, when they feel the author's any one topic book is fun and attract they make decision to buth the strange author whose the topic book from electronic book publisher's platform web store conventiently in short time. Although, they are strangers, they do not know themselves , but the reader can understand what it way that made Google from writing platofrm to create new creative mind and typing network job method to replace traditional hand writing book method for global authors. It will be one kind of new human network writing job.

Hence, global any one reader can apply an innovative search engine , such as google.com to find whether whom author personal new topic books are value to read from internet.

Then, the electroniuc publisher's web store may be new book store platform sale network to help the author to sell many electronic or paper books from electronic network platform

in short time. So, internet may be future new network plaform to help global any one author to create network writing job absolutely. Furthermore, internet may be popular social media

to help any one author to build goold relationship between his/her readers. It is one kind of new network, human network job. New authors do not need to buy many paper books to prepare to put in any one book shop warehouse. Their every book can print on demand to reduce out of book stock in any one book shop. They may choose to sell either electronic books or paper books both from any one book publisher web store. So, electronic network platform may be one kind of good writing channel to help human authors to create income and it can also

help authors to bring new creative mind and new topic fun content books to let readers to know and buy to read from electronic publisher network platform.

Why does human behavior may be one kind of new human network job to bring global economic advantages. ALthough, it may be free income or without inocme, but the person does the network behavior, his/her behavior may be bring advantages to influence many other people's health. For this case, when a worker in a coffee shop in an airport gets a vaccination aganinst the flu, it does not only helps him or her stay healthy, but also helps the many travellers who might otherwise have been inflected if that workers caught the flu.

So, the externality , the result implies the vaccination of even a part of a community conveys benefits to the whole community. For example, governments pay special attention
to the vaccinations of school children, teachers, health mothers, and the elderly, categories of people particularly susceptible not only to catching, but also to transmitting a disease.

It is not accidential that governments are heavily involved with vaccination . When there are externalities, free market, fail to persuade individual incentives with society's
their the worker's decision of whether to get a vaccine ends up attracting whether other people get sick. The workers might not
fully take all these other people's potential suffering into account when making her or his vaccination decision.

As Stanford University does many suggestions, understand this and tries to help them make the right decisions and so providers free flu vaccines for its staff and students.

Small pockets of unvaccinated individuals can allow a disease to gain a spread more widely well-being. For example, parent weighing the costs and benefits of a vaccine for their child is not always thinking of the consequences of that vaccination to other people. THese are markets in which subsidizing or regulating behavior can make everyone better off. Because the reason for requiring that a child be vaccinated before enrolling in school is not just to protect that child, because each child's vaccination affects others via potential contagions.

Robots take our jobs behavioral and economy influences

Robot job behavior brings economy influences

If one day robots can replace human to do simple, even complex jobs. They will bring what influences to our global societial economy.The popular economic refrain declares that the
global middle class is dying and robots will soon take our jobs, e.g. shopping center customer service jobs, library service jobs, cinema ticket sale jobs, restaurant kitchen cooker jobs,
even, bus drivers, taxi drivers etc. public transport driving jobs, accountant, doctors etc. professional jobs. Whether it is beautiful or petty matter if our future societies have many human jobs can be replaced to do from robots. Businessman must may reduce to employ employees and reduce to pay salary or wage, when robots can be replaced to do their employees tasks. But, societies must bring unemployement rate rises , due to societies will have many people loss jobs when their employers choose to buy robots to serve their clients or do any office tasks or customer service or cleaning etc. tasks.

In micro economy view, employers may save money in long term, but in macro economy view, it will cause unemployment ratio rises , even crime rate rises when there are many people lose
jobs in societies. These models of doom, though, fail to account for the hundreds of businesses riding the waves of change in their industries when robots may be invented to replace human to do many simple , even complex tasks in our future societies.

WE may image that one small factory needs to manufacture fishes canes to sell to supermarket, the small , cheaper stuff and higher margin parts of the fishes manufacture industry. Before, this factory needs to employe many human factory workers need to help every fresh customer makeing the perfect fishing gear, designed for performance, durability, and cost in order to achieve to manufacture every fish cane in whole fished processing manufacturing stages. Every worker needs to spend about 15 to twenty minutes to finish every fish cane , till to delivery to any supermarket to sell. If this fish canes manufacturing factory can apply manufacturing robots to help them to finish any one working tasks , every robot can only spend five minutes to finish whole fresh fish cane manufacturing process. Thus, every robot can help this factory save 10 to 15 minutes time to finsh every fish cane manufacturing process. IN fact, time is money, because when every robot can help this factory to reduce 10 to 15 minutes time to compare human worker. Then, this factory can finish about 20 fish canes in one hour if it can use robot to help it to

manufacture fish canes. Otherwise, if this factory still use human workers to help it to manufacture fish canes, then it can finsh about 3 to 4 fish canes in one hour. SO, the manufacturing efficiency ensures that robots must help this fish manufacturing factory to raise fish canes number more than human workers. So, in robotic behavioral economy view, manufacturing robots must help this fish canes manufacturing factory to raise fish canes manufacturing number and deliver increasing number to supermarkets to prepare to sell every day. Robots can help this fish canes manufacturing factory bring manufacturing time saving, rising manufacturing efficiency, improving performance and reducing wages expenditure long time advantages in micro economy view. However, manufacturing robots can also bring disadvanages to society, e.g. increasing unemployment ratio, increasing crime rate,
this factory workers will lose jobs and income, they need earn social welfare from government and increasing government finance pressure in short time, even long time in macro economic view.

Stanford University graduate program in economics, Scott lecturer explained that "in demand and supply economic theory for robots supply and demand case, robots supply number increasing may influence human workers demand number decrease. It sometimes calls " the efficient frontier".

No specific human beings were mentioned in any of economics classes. As robots supply and demand in market case, They (robots) may be purely theoretical " agents" who reached to the most reasonable sale prices in order to persuade any one businessman buyer to make manufacturing robot buying decision whether robots can help him / her to bring how much saving time , saving money, saving cost, improving performance, efficiency economic benefit before he/she plans to reduce workers number when he/she decides to apply robots to replace human workers in his/her factory or office or any service department, e.g. cinema ticket sale service, shopping center customer service, shopping center cleaning , supermarket customer service etc. service or sale tasks. When robots can replace human to do any one of these tasks in any organizations. So, robots may be human worker agents who reached to prices the way robots would react to a software
command. There was nothing that explained why some people thrived and others did n't or why truly brilliant, hardworking people could fail when much lazier folks succeeded." Having been admitted to the Stanford University graduate program in economics, Scott lecturer hoped to get his answers there.

How robots influence our future social changing? Using the right technology can be a boon to your business in this economy. For internet example, it is easier than ever to find well-matched customers
all around the world, to stay in contact with them, and to more quickly design the products they want. If you focus solely on being cutting -edge, though you risk letting the technology
take over what should be very robust relationships with your customers , employees, and colleagues. IN nowaddays society, technoligical advances and cutomation, personal
relationships in business are more crucial than ever. I mean that robots can not replace human to serve clients to let them to feel more comfortable and passion more easily. For shoe shop case example, if the shoe shop apply one robot to serve its clients to replace human shoe salesperson to serve its shoe customers. Robots ensure that they can not persuade every shoe potential buyer to make shoe buying decision more easily when robots need to contact every shoe potential buyer. The reason is simple, because robots can not touch any one shoe buyer individual emotion very easier.

If the shoe buyer needs the robots to help him/her to choose any right shoe styles when he/she can not feel himself / herself can make the most right shoe style choice decision. The robots can not replace human shoe salesperson to make shoe style choice judgement more easily. They must need longer time to analyze whether which shoe style may be the most suitable to the shoe buyer. Otherwise,human shoe salesperson may attempt to make the most right shoe style choice decision to help any one shoe buyer to chooce the most right style shoe because he/ she owns shoe style sale experience, shoe style knowledge, the most important reason is that they can feel every shoe customer individual emotion to touch whether he/she will feel comfortable or happy when they attempt to help every shoe customer to seek the most right shoe style in every shoe customer whole shoe searching processing. Othwerwise, serving robots are only one machine, they can not touch or feel every shoe customer individual emotion whether he/she feel comfortable or unhappy or happy when they need to contact them in whole shoe searching processing. Hence, I believe that some tasks robots can not repalce human staff to do very easily. Otherwise, robots may bring disadvanatges to let any one businessman to loss his/her customers, due to robots can not touch every customer

emotion to compare human staff in service tasks more easily. Robots serving customer behaviors may cause money lose and customers number lose to the shop in micro economic view.

Intellectual human economic behaviors

What does intellectual human economic behaviors mean ? I believe that when we choose or decide to do intellectual behaviors, then our societies will be influenced to bring economic growth in consequence.I shall attempt to indicate pollution case to explain how and why eithet our intellectual or foolish behaviors may bring economic growth or recession in consequence as below:

On one hand, for air pollution social case aspect example, if we only consider to buy cars to drive for working aimr or holiday leisure aim. Then, our societies air will be polluted. Our health will be influenced to bad. Our car driving behaviors may cause global environment air pollution serously. In long tiem, global air pollution will bring our bodies health to be bad. Although, ourselves car driving behaviors may bring our driving travelling leisure enjoyment and comfortable feeling in short time, also we so not need to pay public transport fare often, but we need to compensate ourselves health economic intangible loss due to air pollution , when cars number increases, dirty air will cause ouselves health to become bad.

In the result, we will need to pay more medical expenditure when we are old age, due to ourselves bodies will become bad, due to we breathe global dirty air every day, due to ourselves cars pollute air in long time, e.g. 10 to 20 years, even 30 more without limited air pollution environment. So, driving cars behavior may be one kind of human foolish behavior and our foolish behavior may bring ourselves future long time medical expenditure absolutely.

One the other hand, water pollution social aspect, if we often keep much rubblish to pollute sea, oil exploration porcessing pollute ocean , ships gas pollute ocaen, then fishes will eat polluted food and drive dirty water, due to global ocean is polluted.

In fact, because human only to conside how to buy boats to carry on leisure enjoyment activities, or catch cruises to travel on the sea. Also, oil manufacturers only consider researching anywhere to find new oil exploration places to manufacture oil product, when their oil exploration processes pollute ocarn . Consequently, global fishes drink polluted warer or eat polluted food. They will have poison. SO, human will have high chance to eat poison polluted fishes, due to fishes are poison or are polluted.

So, human is doing foolish activities, we only hope to find oil exploration places to pollute ocean or we only spend money to buy ticket to catch ships to travel anywhere in global ocean. All of these human foolish behaviors will bring pollution to global ocean. On consequently, we will need to compensate to eat polluted or dirty or poision fishes, ourselves bodies health will be bad. In long time, we need have high chance to pay medical expenditure when we are old. So, pollution case may be one good example to explain how and why human foolish behavior may influence ourselves future need to compensate serious medical loss.

All of these human foolish behavior will bring pollution to global ocean. On consequently, we will need to compensate to eat polluted or dirty or poison fished , ourselves bodies health will be bad. In long time, we will have high chance to pay medical expenditure, when we are old. So, pollution case may be one good example to explain how and why human ourselves intellectual or foolish behaviors may influence future long time economic loss or economic growth or recession in micro and micro economic view.

On another water pollution aspect hand, if we often keep rubbish to sea, oil exploration processing pollutes ocean and ships' gas pollute ocean, then fishes will eat polluted food and drink dirty water, due to fishes will eat polluted food and drink dirty sea water because the global ocean is polluted seriously.

In fact, because human only consider how to buy boats to carry on any leisure water activities, or catches cruises to travel on the sea. Also, oil manufacturers only consider any where to find oil exploratin places to manufacture oil products from ocean, when their pol exploration processes can plooute ocean. Consequently, global fishes drink polluted water or eat direty food. They will have poison. So, human will have high chance to eat poison fishes.

Otherwise, such as pollution case, it can infuence inflation or deflation. Consequently, the reason indicates supply and demand theory. If air pollution is serious, then we will consider health issue, global cars demand number may be

influenced to reduce, when global cars number demand will reduce, global car prices and supply number will need to change to fall down in order to attract or persuade global car consumers choose to make car purchase decision.
Hence, global car manufacture number and car price will be influenced to reduce, due to global air pollution issue. Consequently, deflation will occur because when the country citizen usually does not spend much extra saving money to buy car expensive goods. Money value will be low. Otherwise, if global cair pollution is not serious, human considers to buy cars to enjoy driving leisure lives. So, global car demand is influenced to increase , also global car price will also influenced to increase.
Consequently, gobal human will choose to buy cars to drive. Due to we accept to spend extra saving to buy expensive car goods. Car sale price and supply may be influenced to rise up. Money value is influenced to reduce. Inflation may be influenced, due to global car consumers number increases, we would not have extra money to spend easily. Car expensive goods expenditure influences our spending habit to avoid to make car purchase decision more easily. So, human intellectual or foolish activities may bring inflation or deflation consequency in possible indirectly in macro economic view.
On conclusion, above pollution case explain that how and why human intellectual or foolish economic behaviors may bring inflation or deflation consequency as wll as economic growth or recession consequency as well as any goods demand and supply increasing or decreasing consequency. It implies that human behavior may have indirect relationship to influence any goods demand and supply number to either increase or decrease result as well as any goods price will be influenced to increase or decrease in micro and macro economic view.

9 798887 726243

Printed by Libri Plureos GmbH in Hamburg,
Germany